World trademarks and logotypes

World trademarks and logotypes

Edited by
Takenobu Igarashi

Graphic-sha Publishing Company
Tokyo

ISBN 4-7661-0290-8

Manufactured in Japan

First Edition October 1983

Graphic-sha Publishing Co., Ltd.
1-9-12 Kudan-kita Chiyoda-ku
Tokyo 102 Japan

The Attraction of Creating Forms and Images

To publish a book containing world trademarks and logotypes has been one of my goals for many years standing.

As a designer, my work on the design of many symbols has made me acutely aware of the difficulty of forming something into a symbol or sign. At the same time, it is also true that as a professional I have experienced the joy of creating forms and images on a sophisticated level.

The larger a company is, the greater is the influence of its trademark on society, and also that much greater is the responsibility of the designer. To design a trademark as the face of a company incorporating its history, doctrine or policy within the form is in itself a challenging task with great possibilities.

Recently the spread of information and internationalization which are advancing rapidly on a world-wide level, have begun to show their effects in the world of design.

For instance, a trademark is not designed on the basis of the sensibility of one designer, but the direction that the theme and form will take depend on a more analytical interpretation based on scientific research and management strategy considerations, and the trademark and logotype are developed through teamwork. This system has begun to become firmly established as an effective means to avoid difficulties in international trademark registration.

Furthermore, in order for the developed trademark and logotype to be asked to function more effectively, a design system is prepared, and various applicati   s of the basic design are also worked out. As a result, the company image as a whole is more clearly and more strongly established. I basically approve of this methodology, but at times I feel that I would like to give due consideration to ethnic characteristics and high level designs which tend to become lost in the process. That is, I would like to

see trademarks and logotypes themselves retaining cultural value as beautiful forms and images.

The world of trademarks and logotypes, is a world of visual images of condensed information. The collection of such forms in one book was for me more the creation of an interesting picture book than of a valuable resource material. In these trademarks and logotypes, one can read the living ethnic characteristics, social conditions, and the breath of the country, culture and age. In these trademarks and logotypes I felt I was seeing the real world of modern symbols.

Top-level designers participated as advisers in the collection and selection of works for this book. They are works of the highest level designed in various countries during the past 15 years. As all the pages are printed in color, I am confident that it will be very effective as material documentation.

In conclusion, I would like to take this opportunity to express my heartfelt thanks to the many people who cooperated in the publication of this book.

© Takenobu Igarashi
August 17, 1983

Design: A Strategic Synthesis

Design, in which corporate identity, trademarks and logotypes are major examples of the state of the art, is becoming increasingly complex from both an analytical planning and executional standpoint.

As corporations have become more complex, their markets more sophisticated, their competition more aggressive and identity design more common, design as a vehicle of corporate positioning has responded with increasingly more elaborate and complex solutions.

In this era of growing emphasis on the value of corporate communication, trademarks and logotypes play an even greater role in competing for market share.

The process of creating corporate identity design has become highly specialized. Many analytical assessment methods, sophisticated research and marketing techniques are employed.

The designer of today must be well versed in these techniques in order to interface as a consultant with a highly specialized management team and assess corporate objectives. The insight gained from this process must be creatively translated into a highly simplified and well crafted visual statement, expressing a distinctive visual identity, corporate personality, and strategic positioning. The visual identity system developed must be capable of consistent widespread implementation often in many geographical areas with little ongoing design involvement. This is accomplished utilizing elaborate detailed specifications and guidelines.

Successful corporate identity design can and should be a strategic management tool. It can unify a diverse group of companies, reposition a corporation, redefine its markets, provide new life to its products, improve communications, increase public awareness and provide a renewed personality.

Striving for originality, many identity solutions employ a great deal of visual experimentation. This results in many applications which are highly stylistic, which often mask the actual corporate message creating confusion rather than clarification. Design as a cosmetic to corporate positioning can be visually pleasing to the designer but it seldom addresses the real communication requirements of the problem.

Truly successful trademark and logotype design is, and must continue to be, a synthesis. It must be the result of strategic analysis, inspired creativity, dedicated attention to visual detail and consistancy of implementation.

© Stuart Ash·
Gottschalk + Ash International 1983

Thoughts on Logotypes and Symbols

To discuss symbols and logotypes means entering a very complex — often even confused and confusing — territory. Communication and information theory, semiotics and semiology, psychology and psychoanalysis, all make pertinent references to this field; the deeper the study the more complexity and the less clarity.

For the purpose of this short article I offer these definitions:
1: A logotype is the name of a person, a firm .or a product in initials or fully spelled out, designed in such a way that it can be legally registered and protected as a design *bearing in mind that logotypes made up of letters from an existing alphabet will not qualify.* Only a uniqueness of constellation and/or form of letters will result in a valid logotype.
2: A symbol *according to the Oxford Dictionary* is a 'thing regarded by general consent as naturally typifying or representing or recalling something by possession of analogous qualities or by association in fact or thought the colour white, the lion, the thunderbolt, the cross, are symbols of purity, courage, Zeus, Christianity; . . . Mark or character taken as the conventional sign of some object or idea or process, e.g. the astronomical signs for the planets, the letters standing for chemical elements, letters of the alphabet, the mathematical signs for addition and infinity, the asterisk: . . .'

Logotypes and symbols are both signs. Roland Barthes, one of the most important writers on semiology, states 'Semiology postulates a relation between three terms, a signifier and a signified and a sign. The sign is the associative total of the first two terms.' The signifier expresses the signified by a sign. In communication terms: the sender *signifier* encodes the contents of the message *the signified* which is received by the target public *to be defined from case,* which — hopefully — sees it, understands it and acts on it.

Target public means the people for whom the sign should mean something. Very often a sign system need only be understood by one group of people. There is no need for pedestrians to understand transport signs addressed to motorists. Railway signals need only be understood by train drivers and not by pedestrians, passengers or motorists. Signs on office or agricultural machinery need only be understood by those who use and maintain them. The general public is only being addressed for purposes of general information *e.g. hospital sign systems, general danger warnings, etc.* and for sales promotion *commerce, industry, services.* In every case the system has to be learned to be understood. R. Arnheim writes 'the three terms, pictures, symbol, sign do not stand for kinds of images. They rather describe three functions fulfilled by images . . . as a rule the image itself does not tell which function is intended . . . A triangle may be a sign of danger or a picture of a mountain or a symbol of hierarchy. . . To the extent to which images are signs they can serve only as indirect media, for they operate as mere references to the things for which they stand . . .'

Rudolf Modley notes that 'a traffic sign showing a pedestrian in Western clothing may be puzzling or unwelcome to drivers in a non-Western country and that the picture of an old-fashioned locomotive may let a driver of the young generation expect a museum of historical railroad engines rather than a crossing. . .' Commercial trademark designers cannot make their designs self-explanatory. The taste and style of our time associates successful business with clean-cut, starkly reduced shape, and the disorder and rapidity of modern living calls for stimuli of split-second efficiency.'

Frequency of exposure helps recognition. Conversely an excellent symbol design, shown infrequently, is unlikely to be recognized and therefore adds to visual noise and makes for confusion. 'Identification can only be obtained by what the men in the trade call 'strong penetration,' that is, insistent reinforcement of the association of signifier and referent, as

Bibliography   Rudolf Arnheim:'Visual Thinking' *California University Press*
Roland Barthes: 'Mythologies' *Paladin Books*

exemplified by religious emblems *Cross, Star of David*, flag designs *Canada's maple leaf, Japan's rising sun,* or the Red Cross. Therefore, to test the value of trademarks independently of the context that ties them to their owners is like evaluating a diagram on the classroom blackboard without reference to the professor's explanatory speech.' Earlier trademarks attempted to symbolise products or activities. As larger industries become increasingly diversified their symbols can become an obstruction to communication. Cigarette manufacturers may diversify into, for example, cosmetics, food and hotels so that a common visual symbol is no longer apt. This explains the quantity of abstract symbols of recent years of which the best are the basic circle, triangle, square and rectangle or a combination of them. There has been a proliferation of geometric signs adding to each other's confusion. Only those with the most frequent exposure have a chance of being recognised *this development led me to entitle an article in the 1969 Penrose Annual: 'Semiotics or semi-idiotics.'*

Another consequence of this development was the need to add a logotype or at least a word reference to each symbol. As a result, two elements had to be put across instead of one. As space and attention has to be bought expensively, it is easier for one element to register than for two, both in terms of perception and memory. Experienced communicators were quick to realise this problem and, confronted with the choice to do without logotypes or symbols, they had to opt for retaining logotypes at the price of abandoning symbols. This naturally led to the decision to make the name into a logotype/symbol: recognisable words or initials presented in a unique manner *Olivetti, Siemens, RCA, Mobil.* In the case of MOBIL the red pegasus retained only its colour as it was abstracted into the red O within the sequence blue M BIL. I realised the power of this abstraction, combined with its frequent worldwide exposure, when I deciphered Mobil's sign in Egypt: the logo-

type in Arabic, reading from right to left *blue/red/blue/blue/blue*, left me in no doubt of the message.

The exception to this rule are symbols for causes, charitable, political or cultural, when symbols have to have an emotional, dynamic appeal in order to function. They must have abstract qualities to make a first impact yet combine them with sufficient emotional associations.

Roch's proposal of an emblem for the Canadian World Fair 1967 and Bass's symbol for the Committee for Sane Nuclear Policy reduces the objects they depict to simply defined visual patterns. Roch's design illustrates the exhibition theme 'Men and His World'. Bass shows protective hands trying to contain a nuclear explosion.

To conclude these few thoughts I feel that at all times the communication needs must be given priority over artistic, aesthetic considerations. For this reason I am convinced that, for instance, sign systems and symbols at international airports need to be identical rather than different — even if they achieve individual aesthetic results. Airports and their sign systems are for air travellers and taking off in Tokyo to land in Los Angeles, New York, London, Paris or Rome what matters is that the same information is conveyed in the same manner in all these places rather than one or the other having better colour on their signs with a crisper alphabet or a more ingenious symbol system. The total airport information system, worldwide, must possess clear continuity of visual information. This leaves plenty of opportunities for individual expression in architecture, in interior design and in imaginative handling of passenger areas. This may be bad news for the designers but good news for the travellers.

9

Contents

A collection of international symbols
and their applications

All symbols and their applications were produced and applied in the past 15 years.

Credit format:

Technics ——————— Project name
All-Star Band Awards ——————— Business activities
Spencer/Francey (Fifty ——————— Name of design firm
Fingers Incorporated)
Designers: Paul Hodgson, ——————— Name of designers
Stephan Yeates
Toronto, Canada ——————— City and Country of designers

Chapter I

North America

Canada

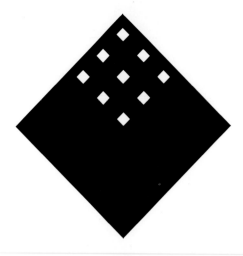

Technics
All-Star Band Awards
Spencer/Francey
(Fifty Fingers Inc.)
Designers: Paul Hodgson,
Stephen Yeates
Toronto, Canada

This symbol is the unifying
element of an annual
awards program mounted
by Technics, a brand of hi-fi
equipment marketed by
Matsushita Electric of
Canada Ltd.; given to outstanding Canadian musical
performers in nine separate
categories. Based on a re-
curring geometric theme,
the nine element unit re-
presents the body of win-
ning performers (dubbed
the 'All-Star Band'), and its
orientation at the apex of
the diamond shaped device
indicates their status within the music industry.

1

vip

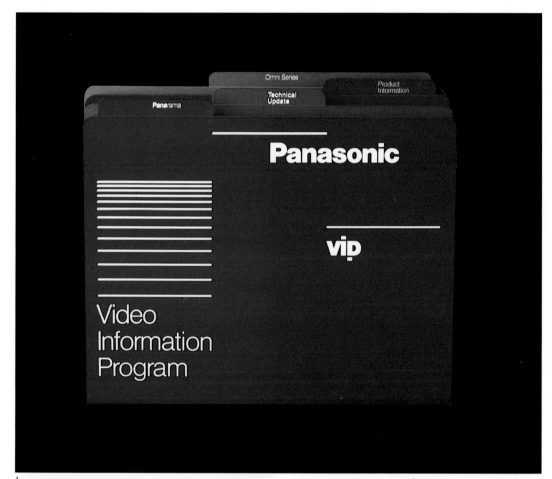

VIP
Panasonic Canada Video
Information Program
Spencer/Francey
(Fifty Fingers Inc.)
Designer: Gary Ludwig
Toronto, Canada

The identification program
was developed for an
ongoing print communi-
cations package for
Panasonic's video equip-
ment dealer network. The
acronym stand for
Video Information Program
while simultaneously
reflecting the better known
meaning of VIP to highlight
the importance of the
dealers to the operation.

1

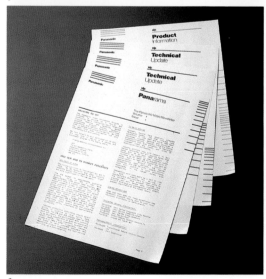

2

3

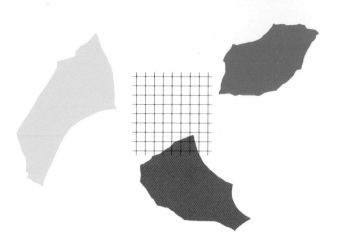

Dundas Valley
School of Art
Canadian art school
Spencer/Francey
(Fifty Fingers Inc.)
Designer: Paul Hodgson
Toronto, Canada

This visual identity was
implemented in conjunc-
tion with the school's
newly structured curricu-
lum. It is a positive
affirmation of the seem-
ingly contradictory idea of
individual artistic effort
being encouraged and
developed within a
controlled environment.

d

21 Ogilvie Street
Dundas, Ontario
Canada L9H 2S1
(416) 628-6357

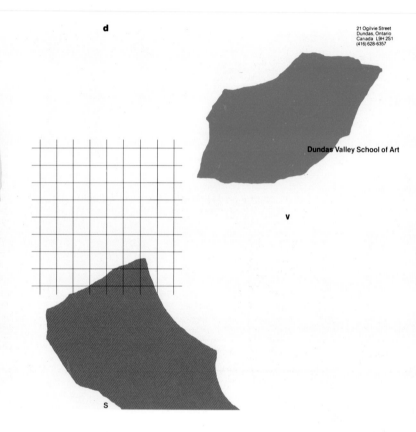

Dundas Valley School of Art

v

S

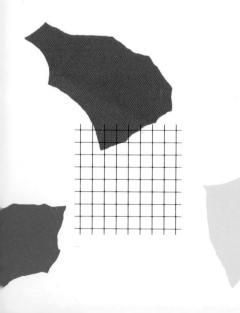

Litho Associates 509 Stinson Road
St. Laurent   Quebec
Telephone
514 744-4933

Litho Associates
509 Stinson Road
St. Laurent
Quebec

Estimate

1

Litho Associates
509 Stinson Road, St. Laurent
Quebec
Tel. (514) 744-4933

James P. Gearey
President

2

Litho Associates
Printing firm
Gottschalk + Ash
International
Designers: Fritz Gottschalk,
Fredy Jaggi
Montreal, Canada

Gottschalk + Ash Montreal
were hired to develop this
visual identity program for
a Montreal printing firm
for use on printed and
promotional material.
The emphasis when devel-
oping the symbol was
placed on creating the
feeling of the traditional
and the new.

Parc Belmont
Amusement park
Gottschalk + Ash
International
Designers: Peter Steiner,
Michael Friedland
Montreal, Canada

A new visual identity
program for an existing
Montreal amusement park
was developed for use
on printed material,
signage, equipment and
various other promo-
tional material.

1

2

PARC BELMONT

BON D'ESCOMPTE

$ **1.**

DISCOUNT COUPON

Obtenez avec chaque achat un bon qui vous donne droit à $1 d'escompte sur le prix d'entrée régulier, comprenant tous les manèges (sauf le karting), les attractions (sauf le spectacle de prestidigitation) et des spectacles quotidiens. On ne peut utiliser qu'un seul bon par billet.
Le Parc Belmont est ouvert les week-ends à compter du 26 avril, tous les jours du 1er juin au 1er septembre et les week-ends des 6-7 et 13-14 septembre

Get a coupon here with each purchase entitling you to a $1 discount on the regular admission price, which also covers every ride (except go-carts) and all attractions (except the illusion show), daily entertainment included. Only one such coupon may be used per admission ticket.
Parc Belmont is open weekends starting April 26, daily from June 1 until September 1, plus the weekends of September 6-7 and 13-14

Design Gottschalk + Ash / Imprimerie AGS Printing

3

4

5

Spence Bay
Eskimo Co-operative
Gottschalk + Ash
International
Designers: Fritz Gottschalk,
Michael Friedland
Montreal, Canada

Spence Bay
ᑳᐅᐊ

1

"We design things "the Down Souths" might like. You have to think about two things, one Inuit and one Down South, and somehow put them together. We use our ideas not only to make things for the South, but for ourselves too. I like that."
Quotation from "Anaoyok" of Spence Bay

Traditional crafts are best explained as those crafts which the Inuit have always done as part of their way of life and upon which their survival has often depended. They are regarded as important contributions to Canadian culture and heritage.
The products of Spence Bay are designed and made by the Inuit people who have much to share with others. The shop, known as *arnaqarvik* "the place where the women gather", is a very central point of Spence Bay, a community of 400 people on Boothia Peninsula in the Central Arctic.

«Nous faisons des choses qui pourraient plaire aux «gens du Sud». Il faut penser aux deux, les Inuit et les gens du Sud, et les mettre ensemble de quelque façon. Nous cherchons des idées non seulement pour les gens du Sud mais pour nous-mêmes aussi. J'aime cela.»
Citation de «Anaoyok» de Spence Bay

Les métiers traditionnels sont ceux que les Inuit ont toujours exercé dans leur vie, ceux dont leur survivance dépendait souvent. Ils sont considérés comme des apports importants à la culture et au patrimoine canadien.
Les produits de Spence Bay sont conçus et fabriqués par un peuple qui a beaucoup à partager avec les autres. L'atelier s'appelle *arnaqarvik*, «le lieu de réunion des femmes». Il est au cœur de Spence Bay, petite agglomération de 400 personnes établie sur la péninsule Boothia, au centre de l'Arctique canadien.

Talcoya
Spence Bay
N.W.T.
X0E 1B0
Canada

2

Canexus
Canadian Business
Equipment Manufacturers
Association
Gottschalk + Ash
International
Designers: Gottschalk +
Ash International,
Les Holloway
Toronto, Canada

1

2

SEC∪RITY

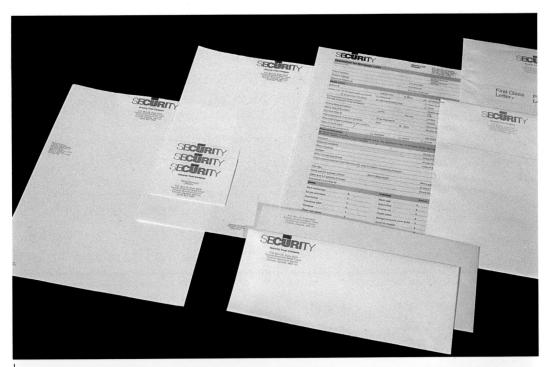

Security
Trust company
Gottschalk + Ash
International
Designers: Peter Adam,
Stuart Ash
Toronto, Canada

1

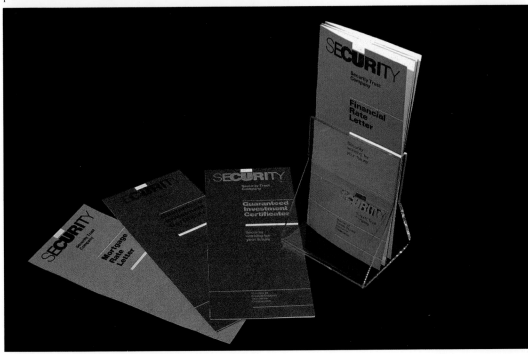

2

Claude Neon
Electrical sign
manufacturer
Gottschalk + Ash
International
Designers: Stuart Ash,
Fredy Jaggi,
Fritz Gottschalk
Toronto, Canada

2

3

Yonge
Toronto City Planning
Gottschalk + Ash
International
Designers: Gottschalk +
Ash International, Les
Holloway
Toronto, Canada

**Centennial of
Confederation**
Canadian Government
Centennial
Gottschalk + Ash
International
Designer: Stuart Ash
Toronto, Canada

Maclean Hunter
Communications
corporation
Gottschalk + Ash
International
Designer: Stuart Ash
Toronto, Canada

DI Design
Graphic design firm
Gottschalk + Ash
International
Designer: Stuart Ash
Toronto, Canada

26

The Metric Song / La chanson métrique

Metric Conversion Canada
Gottschalk + Ash International
Designer: Stuart Ash
Toronto, Canada

CBC
Canadian Broadcasting
Corporation
Burton Kramer Assoc. Ltd.
Designer: Burton Kramer
Toronto, Canada

The Canadian Broadcast-
ing Corporation/Société
Radio-Canada (in French
speaking Canada) is the
national broadcasting
service, including both
television and radio with
an overseas service named
Radio Canada Internation-
al.

A symbol-logo was
designed by Kramer
Associates along with a
comprehensive visual
identity program for the
corporation. The symbol
and programs are
extremely visible daily to
millions of Canadians, on
their television sets, on
CBC vehicles, cameras,
banners and flags, publications and records, and
building identification.

A graphic standards
manual has been written,
designed and produced for
the corporation by Kramer
Associates. It contains the
background and philoso-
phy, master art, specifications and basic
information for the pro-
duction and maintenance
for all aspects of the visual
identity program. The
design program went
beyond visual identifica-
tion only, with
supplementary radio on-
air programs.

Canadian
Broadcasting
Corporation

Société
Radio-
Canada

Visual Identification
Program

Programme d'identification
visuelle

2

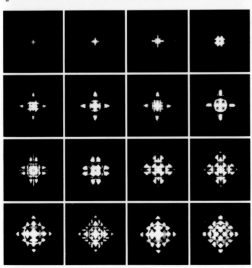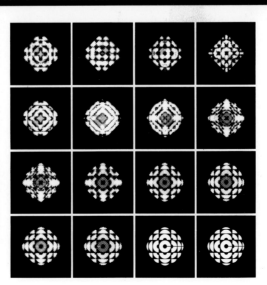

3

5

First Choice! CBC Radio & Television

6

7

8

Hornpayne Center
Community development
program
Burton Kramer Assoc. Ltd.
Designer: Burton Kramer
Toronto, Canada

Hornepayne is a northern
Ontario town of some
1800 inhabitants. It is a
major maintenance
point for the Canadian
National Railways between
Toronto, Montreal and
Winnipeg, where the
winters are severe.

Kramer Associates has
designed a symbol-logo for
this center which includes
all signs and graphics,
interior and exterior, three
dimensional graphics
for the major pylon and
wall graphics for the mall
and high school. Other
applications include,
signage for motorists,
graphics for the center's
sport facilities, hotel,
coffee shop and fast food
outlets.

Centre Inn

Hornepayne, Ontario

Mexico

INVITACION

CONMEMORACION
DEL XXV
ANIVERSARIO DEL
BANCO NACIONAL
DE CUBA

27 AL 30 DE OCTUBRE 1975

National Bank of Cuba
Anniversary of the National
Bank of Cuba
Félix Beltrán Studio
Designers: Félix Beltrán,
Jorge Fornés
Mexico City, Mexico

2

CONMEMORACION DEL XXV ANIVERSARIO DEL BANCO NACIONAL DE CUBA

1

Cimex Corporation
Import/export enterprise
Félix Beltrán Studio
Designers: Félix Beltrán,
Dagoberto Marcelo
Mexico City, Mexico

Henry Weinhardt
Brewing company
Primo Angeli Graphics
Designer: Primo Angeli
San Francisco, USA

3

4

1

2

5

6

GRID

Grid
Computer systems
Primo Angeli Graphics
Designer: Primo Angeli
San Francisco, USA

1

2

MIN🔵LTA

1

2

Minolta
Camera company
Saul Bass/Herb Yager and
Associates
Designers: Saul Bass,
Art Goodman, Saul Bass/
Herb Yager and Associates
Hollywood, USA

MINOLTA

3

AT&T

AT&T
American Telephone and
Telegraph
Saul Bass/Herb Yager and
Associates
Designer: Saul Bass
Hollywood, USA

In 1968, AT&T management
acknowledged the need
for change as well as unifi-
cation of the 23 regional
companies that comprise
the Bell System. The
program was structured
into five phases of work,
ranging from the initial
step of orientation and
study, to the development
of a new trademark sys-
tem, applications, and
control documents that
would help implement
and maintain the program.

The sheer physical size of
the task was extraordinary.
It was, at the time the
largest corporate identification program ever under-
taken. Today virtually
the entire Bell System fleet
now displays the new
identification. Bell System
building identification
and signage today
encompasses exterior and
interior signage for more
than 30,000 buildings.
Implementation of the program is still going on.

1

2

3

Warner Communications

Saul Bass/Herb Yager and Associates
Designers: Saul Bass, Art Goodman, Saul Bass/Herb Yager and Associates
Hollywood, USA

Warner Communications interests involve music publishing, records, motion picture and television film production and distribution, book and magazine publishing, and cable television. Because of the wide variety of companies sharing the venerable Warner Bros. shield, a coherent identity program that could be used by all divisions was developed by Saul Bass/Herb Yager and Associates in 1972. The key element in the new corporate and divisional identificational system was a new symbol that suggested the letter 'W', somewhat electronic in character, which conveyed the communications focus of the corporation.

1. Headquarters flag of Warner Communications, Inc.
2. Building interior signage

1

2

United Airlines

Saul Bass/Herb Yager and Associates
Designers: Saul Bass, Art Goodman, Mamoru Shimokochi
Hollywood, USA

GIRL SCOUTS

Girl Scouts of America
Saul Bass/Herb Yager and
Associates
Designers: Saul Bass,
Art Goodman,
Saul Bass/Herb
Yager and Associates
Hollywood, USA

The new face of Girl Scouting

Generations
Behavioral medicine
clinic
Design Collaborative
Designer: Richard F. Dahn
Seattle, USA

2

1

Shangri-la Hotel
Dyer/Kahn Inc.
Designers: Rod Dyer,
Clive Pearcy
Los Angeles, USA

HOTEL SHANGRI-LA

1301 OCEAN AVE., SANTA MONICA, CALIFORNIA 90401 (213) 394-2791 TLX: 182091

SelecTV
Cable television network
Dyer/Kahn Inc.
Designers: Rod Dyer,
Hoi Ping Law
Los Angeles, USA

Eagle Records
Recording studio
Dyer/Kahn Inc.
Designer: Rod Dyer
Los Angeles, USA

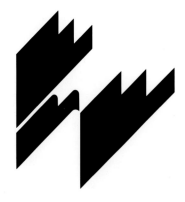

Eagle Records

Patti's Productions
TV productions
Dyer/Kahn Inc.
Designers: Rod Dyer,
Andy Engel
Los Angeles, USA

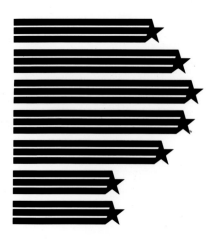

Carolco
Motion picture distributor
Dyer/Kahn Inc.
Designer: Rod Dyer
Los Angeles, USA

BERNARD'S

Bernard's
Restaurant
John Follis & Associates
Designers: John Follis,
Wayne Hunt
Los Angeles, USA

1

BERNARD'S

Les Hors D'Oeuvres

La Terrine de Canard au Poivre Vert	3.50
Plate of Duck with Green Peppercorn from Madagascar	
Le Saumon Fumé D'Irlande	4.50
Smoked Salmon from Ireland	
Le Foie Gras au Naturel	8.00
Goose Liver au Naturel	
Le Cocktail de Homard Frais	7.00
Cocktail of Fresh Maine Lobster and Pineapple	
Le Jambon Fumé aux Fruits de Saison	4.50
Prosciutto Ham Served with Fruit of the Season	
Le Melon au Porto	3.00
Fresh Melon marinated in Port Wine	
Le Cocktail de Crevettes Rilievre	4.00
Cocktail of Shrimp Served on Half Avocado	
Le Caviar au Naturel	per ounce 12.50
L'Assiette de Hors D'Oeuvres Varies	4.00
Assortment of Fresh Cold Hors D'Oeuvres	

Les Potages

La Bisque au Crabe	3.00
Bisque of Fresh Crab	
La Gratinée des Halles	2.00
Our Chef's Version of the French Onion Soup	
La Crème d'Avocat Glacée	2.50
Iced Cream of Avocado	

Les Salades

La Salade a la Moutarde a l'Orange	2.00
Salad of Greens with Orange Flavored Dressing	
La Salade des Gourmets	3.00
Salad of Hearts of Palms, Fresh Mushrooms, Tomatoes, Lettuce and Shallots	
La Salade de Cresson au Citron	2.50
Salad of Watercress Served with Fresh Lemon Dressing	

Les Poissons et Crustaces Frais

Le Red Snapper Grille Beurre Blanc	8.50
Broiled Red Snapper Fillet with White Butter Sauce	
Le Filet de Sole Tout Paris	10.00
Poached Fresh Fillet of Sole Served with a White Wine and Lobster Americaine Sauce	
Le Filet de Sanddah Grenobloise	8.50
Fresh Sanddah Saute with Lemon and Capers	
Le Filet de Loup de Mer Au Vin Rouge	9.00
Fillet of Striped Bass Served with a Delicate Red Wine Sauce	
Le Civet de Langouste du Pacifique	14.00
Fresh Pacific Lobster Stewed in a Red Wine Sauce	

Les Poissons et Crustaces Importes

La Coquille de Fruit de Mer Parisienne	8.00
Scallops, Shrimps, Crabmeat with Veloute Sauce	
La Quenelle de Brochet Nantua	8.00
Quenelle of Pike Cooked in a Lobster Sauce	
La Darne de Saumon au Champagne	9.00
Poached Salmon Steak with a Champagne Veloute Sauce	
Le Turbot Poche Sauce Paloise	10.00
Poached Turbot Served with a Minted Bearnaise Sauce	
Notre Specialities	10.00
La Bouillabaisse Marseillaise	

Les Viandes

L'Escalope de Veau Normande	10.00
Medallions of Veal Sauteed and Served with Fresh Apples	
L'Entrecote de Boeuf Grille Maitre D'	12.50
Charcoal Broiled New York Cut Served with Maitre d'Butter	
Le Coeur de Filet aux Herbes de Provence	12.50
Charcoal Broiled Filet Mignon with Aromatic Herbs	
Les Noisettes d'Agneau a L'Estragon	12.50
Medallions of Lamb Sauteed, Fresh Tarragon Sauce	

2

Al's Garage
Clothing store
John Follis & Associates
Designers: John Follis,
Constance Beck
Los Angeles, USA

1

2

3

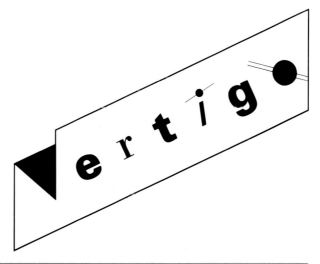

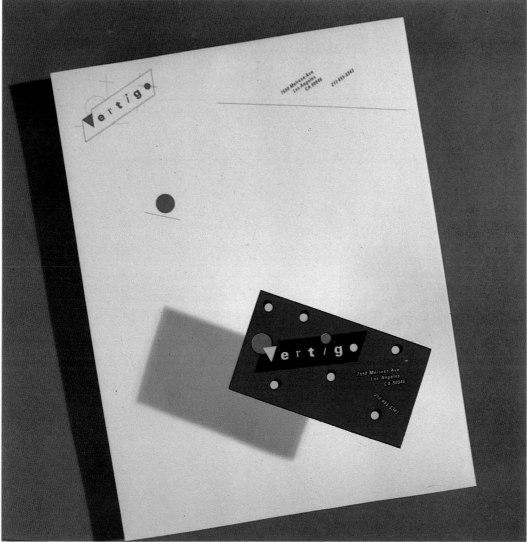

Vertigo
Retailer
April Greiman Studio
Designer: April Greiman,
Jayme Odgers
Los Angeles, USA

1

2

China Club
Chinese restaurant
April Greiman Studio
Designer: April Greiman
Los Angeles, USA

1

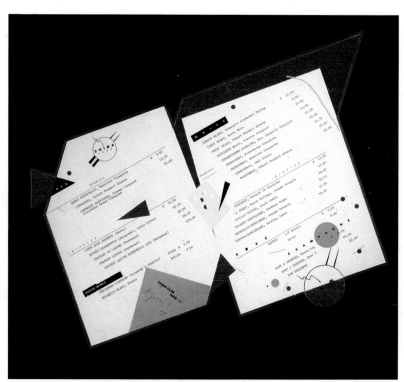

2

3

WINDFARMS

Windfarms
Wind energy company
April Greiman Studio
Designers: April Greiman,
Jayme Odgers
Los Angeles, USA

1

2

3

The Golf Villas

1

2

Kapalua
Resort
Bruce Hopper Design
Designer: Bruce Hopper
Honolulu, USA

Kapalua is a condominium
resort development
built on a former pineapple
plantation on the island
of Maui in Hawaii.

"Land this stunning demands a personal commitment.
And nothing less."
Walt Richardson, Architect
The Golf Villas

Metro (Private) Ltd.
Department store
Landor Associates
Designers: Landor
Associates
San Francisco, USA

Metro (Private) Ltd., is one of the largest and fastest growing department stores in Singapore. They maintain two separate store identities: Metro, a non-speciality, family-style store carrying a large variety of general merchandise items, and Metro Grand, an upscale, top-of-the-line 'boutique' featuring international designer fashions.

Metro retained Landor Associates in 1982, in the midst of tremendous growth and dramatic change throughout Singapore, and in recognition of their need to update their image and unify their variety of unrelated communication elements as part of a long-range marketing plan that calls for expansion of both Metro and Metro Grand stores.

The new 'signature' created by Landor Associates features the initial 'M' rendered in flowing calligraphic form, and retains Metro's bright red color. Enclosed in four square bands of a deeper red, to contain the 'M', provide strength and stability, and complement and soften the intensity of the primary color. The mark retains the original 'chop' signature while making it more contemporary and legible. For Metro Grand, also identified by the new 'M' symbol, a brown and gold color scheme is used for a more sophisticated image. This new signature is bold enough to be effective on exterior signing and on company vehicles and carrybags, yet contains sufficient subtleties to be appropriate when used on garment labels of the finest merchandise.

METRO GRAND

美羅豪華

1

4

2

5

 METRO

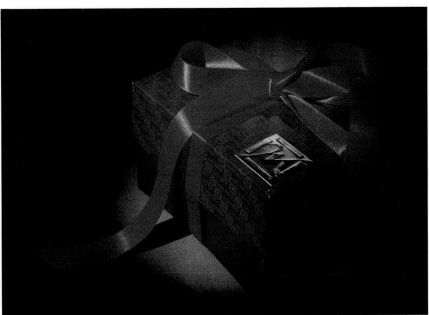

3

6

WESTIN HOTELS

Westin
Western International
Hotels
Landor Associates
Designers: Landor
Associates
San Francisco, USA

Western International
Hotels, America's oldest
operating hotel manage-
ment company, is affiliated
with 55 hotels in 14
countries. With an ambi-
tious expansion program
calling for the addition of
at least 22 hotels and
resorts by 1985, this highly
profitable subsidiary of
UAL Inc. (which is also the
parent company of United
Airlines) retained Landor
Associates in 1980 to
develop an identity whose
clarity and memorability
would better convey the
company-wide dedication
to quality and service,
while also identifying all
the various hotels as
members of the same
group.

Following an extensive
evaluation of the existing
name and identity system,
Landor Associates under-
took a major study for the
new corporate symbol and
the selected new name,
Westin (combining the
initial syllables from both
words, Western and
International). The
resultant signature, with
its shorter, more easily
recognizable name and a
symbol that reflects
graciousness and quality,
provides an immediate
point of reference for all
target audiences. The new
identity will also serve as
a strong unifying element
in media communications,
advertising, exterior and
interior signing, restaurant
and guest room materials,
and employee and
customer related items.

1

2

54

Alitalia

Alitalia Airlines
Landor Associates
Designers: Landor
Associates
San Francisco, USA

Ranked fourth among western world carriers in length of air routes flown, and sixth largest in transatlantic passenger trade, Alitalia of Roma, Italy, was a major factor both within its industry and in terms of impact on the European economy when coming to Landor Associates in 1969. Yet, it was inaccurately thought to be a small, old-fashioned, inefficient domestic carrier; an 'Italian airline for Italians.' To eliminate these negative attributes, an identification system was needed that repositioned Alitalia by successfully projecting not only an up-to-date national image, but a strong international one as well. A modern 'A' letterform symbol became the major component of the new identity, which extended into a logotype, forming a wordmark; the corporation's marketing signature. Inspired by Italy's national colors, a distinctive red, white and green color scheme was implemented throughout the system, including a wide variety of both cargo and passenger aircraft. The result was a communications system which not only improved visual impact and provided consistency, but which also generated increased enthusiasm on the part of the staff, and reduced costs for such items as printed material. The ideology behind this corporate identification program has proven highly successful, especially when measured in terms of undiminished value over the course of more than a decade.

1

2

Hawaii Loa Ridge
Residential development
Clarence Lee Design &
Associates
Designer: Clarence Lee
Honolulu, USA

Hawaii Loa Ridge is a
residential development
located in Honolulu, Hawaii
on a ridge that overlooks
the Pacific Ocean. The
symbol was based on the
entrance to the develop-
ment, which is surrounded
by ridges on both sides.

1

Hnol inc • Davies Pacific Center • Suite 2102 • 841 Bishop Street • Honolulu Hawaii 96813 • Ph: (808) 526-0611

2

1

Jean René
Lingerie store
The Office of Michael
Manwaring
Designers: Michael
Manwaring,
Bill Chiaravalle
San Francisco, USA

2

Oakville Grocery Co.
Gourmet food store
The Office of Michael
Manwaring
Designer: Michael
Manwaring
San Francisco, USA

1

Headlands
Condominium
development
The Office of Michael
Manwaring
Designer: Michael
Manwaring
San Francisco, USA

Ted's
Cocktail lounge
Harry Murphy + Friends
Designers: Harry Murphy,
Diane Levin
Mill Valley, USA

Fine food, spirits and friends.

218 Sir Francis Drake Blvd.
San Anselmo, California
Telephone 453-8600

1

2

vidiom.

Vidiom
Video products outlet
Harry Murphy + Friends
Designers: Harry Murphy,
Stanton Klose
Mill Valley, USA

Vidiom is a retail chain of
video products store.
The three dots always
appear in red, green and
blue — the three primary
colors in the technology of
video transmission.

The Small Things Company
Retail store
Harry Murphy + Friends
Designers: Harry Murphy,
Stanton Klose
Mill Valley, USA

The Small Things Company, is a San Francisco retail and mail order business, which markets floral cachets, pot pourri, jewelry and other small gift items.

These are four of the ten separate symbols that collectively comprise the identity system.

The Small Things Company
P.O. Box 16252
San Francisco, Ca. 94116
Telephone 415 · 564 · 9222

The Small Things Company
P.O. Box 16252
San Francisco, Ca. 94116
Telephone 415 · 564 · 9222

Invoice

1

2

Marin Swim School
Harry Murphy + Friends
Designers: Harry Murphy,
Sheldon Lewis
Mill Valley, USA

This is to certify that

has participated in the

Marin Swim School Swim

Date

Instructor

1

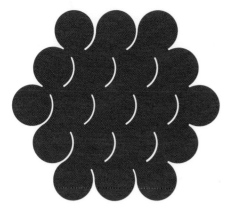

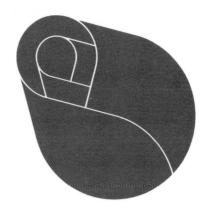

The Small Things Company
P.O. Box 16252
San Francisco, Ca. 94116
Telephone 415 564 9222

The Small Things Company
P.O. Box 16252
San Francisco, Ca. 94116
Telephone 415 564 9222

Purchase Order

Statement

3

4

Marin Swim School
Phone 415 457-5455

Class

Date

Time

2

Marin Swim School

Post Office Box 3646
San Rafael, Ca. 94902
Phone 415 457-5455

Lyn Jensen

4

Parent's Name		Date
Student's		Age
Address	City	Zip
Phone (Day)	(Evening)	
Place of Instruction	Class	Total Due
Class Time	Date	Amount Pre-paid
Referred by	Confirmed	Amount Due

3

Lion & Compass
Restaurant
Gerald Reis & Co.
Designer: Gerald Reis
San Francisco, USA

1

2

Adobe Savings
Savings and loan
Gerald Reis & Co.
Designer: Gerald Reis
San Francisco, USA

FOLKWEAR

Folkwear
Clothing pattern design
and manufacturer
Gerald Reis & Co.
Designers: Gerald Reis,
Gretchen Schields
San Francisco, USA

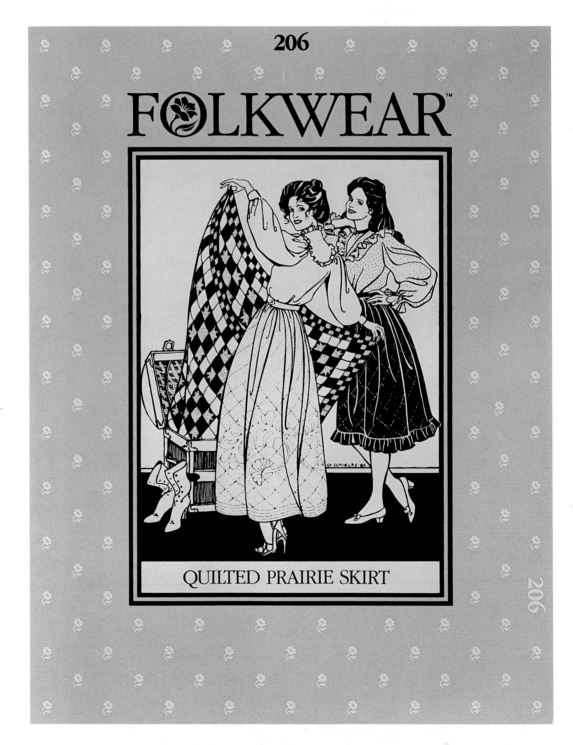

66

A
Guide
To
Stanford
Shopping
Center

**Stanford Shopping
Center**
Gerald Reis & Co.
Designers: Marget Larson,
Gerald Reis
San Francisco, USA

1

2

3

4

Pharmavite
Pharmaceuticals
manufacturer
Robert Miles Runyan &
Associates
Designers: Robert Miles
Runyan & Associates
Playa del Rey, USA

Obunsha
Japanese publisher
Robert Miles Runyan &
Associates
Designers: Robert Miles
Runyan & Associates
Playa del Rey, USA

Unibanco
Mexican bank
Robert Miles Runyan &
Associates
Designers: Robert Miles
Runyan & Associates
Playa del Rey, USA

Crown Zellerbach
Paper company
Robert Miles Runyan &
Associates
Designers: Robert Miles
Runyan & Associates
Playa del Rey, USA

Stars in Motion 2

Winter/1983

1

2

Los Angeles 1984
Olympic Games
Robert Miles Runyan &
Associates
Designers: Robert Miles
Runyan & Associates
Playa del Rey, USA

© 1980 L.A. Olympic Committee

The Symbol

The star is a universal symbol of the highest aspirations of mankind.

The star that symbolizes the Games of the XXIIIrd Olympiad is a star in motion. The horizontal bars portray the speed with which the contestants pursue excellence while the repetition of the star shape connotes the spirit of competition between equally outstanding physical forms.

The symbol colors—blue, white and red —were chosen for their traditional significance in the awarding of prizes for first, second and third place. These colors are also the national colors of the United States of America, and the same three colors appear in the flags of many other countries, while blue and red in combination with other colors are in the flags of additional nations.

The official symbol for the Games of the XXIIIrd Olympiad was designed for the LAOOC by Robert Miles Runyan & Associates.

3

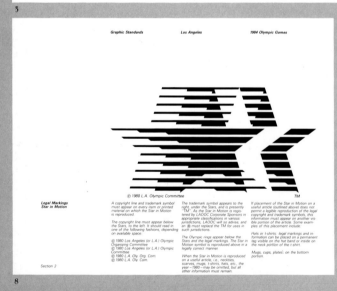

© 1980 L.A. Olympic Committee

TM

Legal Markings Star in Motion

A copyright line and trademark symbol must appear on every item or printed material on which the Star in Motion is reproduced.

The copyright line must appear below the Stars, to the left. It should read in one of the following fashions, depending on available space:

© 1980 Los Angeles for L.A.) Olympic Organizing Committee
© 1980 Los Angeles for L.A.) Olympic Committee
© 1980 L.A. Oly. Org. Com.
© 1980 L.A. Oly. Com.

Section 2

The trademark symbol appears to the right, under the Stars, and is presently "TM". As the Star in Motion is registered by LAOOC Corporate Sponsors in appropriate classifications in various jurisdictions, LAOOC will so advise, and an ® must replace the TM for uses in such jurisdictions.

The Olympic rings appear below the Stars and the legal markings. The Star in Motion symbol is reproduced above in a legally correct manner.

When the Star in Motion is reproduced on a useful article, i.e., neckties, scarves, mugs, t-shirts, hats, etc., the year—1980—may be omitted, but all other information must remain.

If placement of the Star in Motion on a useful article (outlined above) does not permit a legible reproduction of the legal copyright and trademark symbols, this information must appear on another visible portion of the article. Some examples of this placement include:

Hats or t-shirts: legal markings and information can be placed on a permanent tag visible on the hat band or inside on the neck portion of the t-shirt.

Mugs, cups, plates: on the bottom portion

8

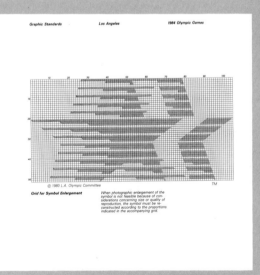

© 1980 L.A. Olympic Committee

TM

Grid for Symbol Enlargement

When photographic enlargement of the symbol is not feasible because of considerations concerning size or quality of reproduction, the symbol must be reconstructed according to the proportions indicated in the accompanying grid.

9

4

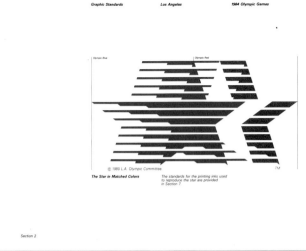

Olympic Blue   Olympic Red

© 1980 L.A. Olympic Committee   TM

The Star in Matched Colors   The standards for the printing inks used to reproduce the star are provided in Section 7.

Section 2

5

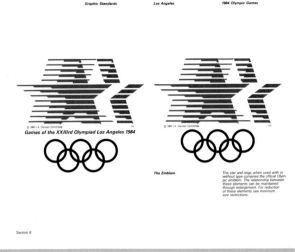

© 1980 L.A. Olympic Committee   © 1980 L.A. Olympic Committee   TM

Games of the XXIIIrd Olympiad Los Angeles 1984

The Emblem   The star and rings when used with or without type comprise the official Olympic emblem. The relationship between these elements can be maintained through enlargement. For reduction of these elements see minimum size restrictions.

Section 6

6

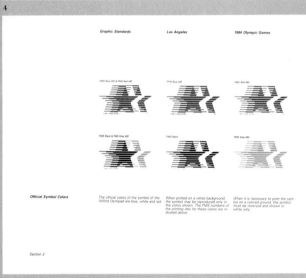

PMS Blue 283 & PMS Red 485   PMS Blue 283   PMS Red 485

PMS Black & PMS Gray 402   PMS Black   PMS Gray 402

Official Symbol Colors   The official colors of the symbol of the XXIIIrd Olympiad are blue, white and red.   When printed on a white background, the symbol may be reproduced only in the colors shown. The PMS numbers of the printing inks for these colors are indicated above.   When it is necessary to print the symbol on a colored ground, the symbol must be reversed and shown in white only.

Section 2

7

© 1980 L.A. Olympic Committee   Games of the XXIIIrd Olympiad Los Angeles 1984

Games of the XXIIIrd Olympiad Los Angeles 1984

Minimum Size Restrictions   When the emblem is produced below 4-1/2 inches in overall width, the above version with extended type is to be used. The small emblem shown is the smallest allowed version.

Section 6

10

Los Angeles Olympic Organizing Committee

Los Angeles, California 90084 USA
Telephone (213) 209-1984
Telex: 194694 • (Int'l) 4720482

Games of the XXIIIrd Olympiad Los Angeles July 28 to August 12, 1984

Wold Communications
Thomas & Associates
Designer: Gregory Thomas
Los Angeles, USA

Robert Wold Company arranges production, distribution and interconnection for broadcasting TV, cable and pay-TV, radio and video-conferencing via satellites.

Wold had originally gone to a large design office for a logotype and corporate program. Some five months after it was created, Wold contacted Thomas & Associates to redesign the entire program and logotype. Applications also include satellite dishes, on-air promotions, etc..

Robert Wold Company, Inc.

10880 Wilshire Boulevard
Los Angeles, California 90024

(213) 474-3500
TWX 910-342-6977

Robert Wold Companys, Inc.

10880 Wilshire Boulevard
Suite 2204
Los Angeles, CA 90024

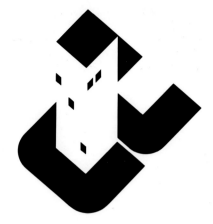

International Cleaning Contractors
Thomas & Associates
Designer: Gregory Thomas
Los Angeles, USA

International Cleaning Contractors is an office maintenance company that specializes in the upkeep and operations of buildings.

WOLD
Robert Wold Company, Inc.

Videocassette

Robert Wold Company, Inc.

WOLD

10880 Wilshire Boulevard
Suite 2204
Los Angeles, CA 90024

(213) 474-3600
TWX 910-342-6977

2

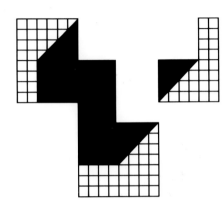

Teletech
Computer answering service
Thomas & Associates
Designer: Gregory Thomas
Los Angeles, USA

San Marino Bank
Thomas & Associates
Designer: Gregory Thomas
Los Angeles, USA

Working with John Klein of Klein Advertising, Thomas & Associates developed this symbol for the bank.

Los Angeles International Film Exposition
Thomas & Associates
Designer: Gregory Thomas
Los Angeles, USA

VEU
Subscription television
Thomas & Associates
Designers: Gregory
Thomas, B. Reynolds
Los Angeles, USA

VEU (Video Entertainment
Unlimited) is a pay-
subscription television
service developed by
Golden West Broadcasters
(KTLA) in Los Angeles, for
distribution in the mid-
west.

Thomas & Associates
developed the tradename
and logotype as well as
manual, signage, on-air
graphics, and monthly TV
guide.

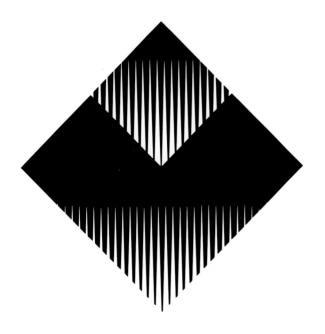

Light Inc.
Photo lab
Urano Design Inc.
Designers: Ryo Urano,
Lester Yamamoto
Honolulu, USA

Venture Graphics
Graphic communication
service company
Vanderbyl Design
Designers: Michael
Vanderbyl,
Vanderbyl Design
San Francisco, USA

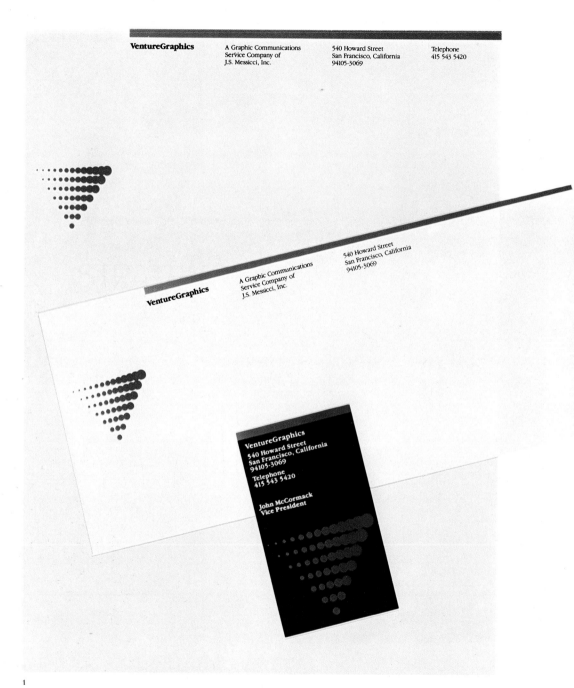

1

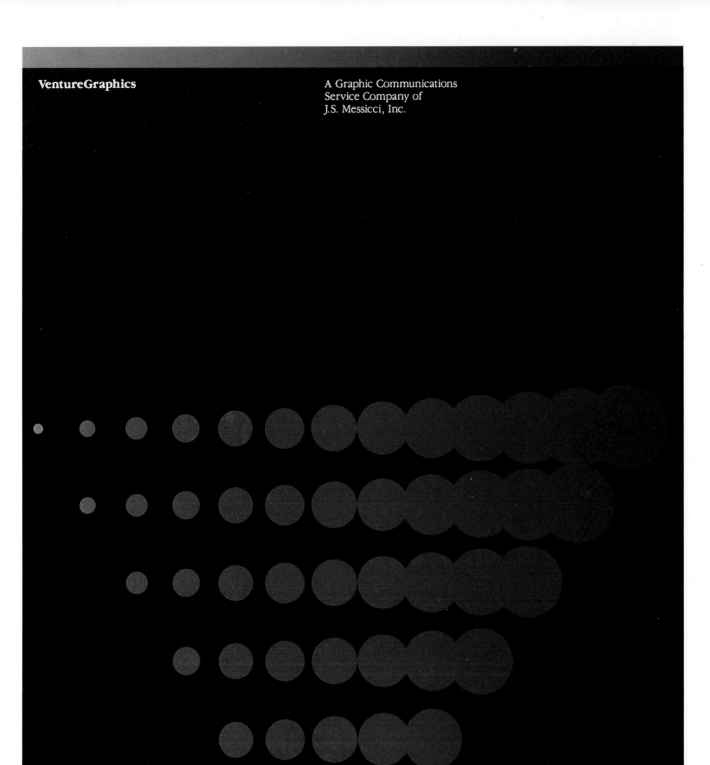

VentureGraphics

A Graphic Communications
Service Company of
J.S. Messicci, Inc.

2

Bankers Trust
Vanderbyl Design
Designers: Michael
Vanderbyl,
Vanderbyl Design
San Francisco, USA

Smith + Schraishuhn
Architectural firm
Vanderbyl Design
Designers: Michael
Vanderbyl,
Vanderbyl Design
San Francisco, USA

Marina Bay
Planned community
development
Vanderbyl Design
Designers: Michael
Vanderbyl,
Vanderbyl Design
San Francisco, USA

The Court
Handball court chain
Vanderbyl Design
Designers: Michael
Vanderbyl,
Vanderbyl Design
San Francisco, USA

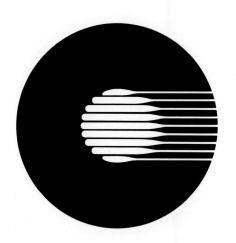

Citrans
Corporate transportation
and warehousing service
Vanderbyl Design
Designers: Michael
Vanderbyl,
Vanderbyl Design
San Francisco, USA

Canyon Lakes
Real estate development
Vanderbyl Design
Designers: Michael
Vanderbyl,
Vanderbyl Design
San Francisco, USA

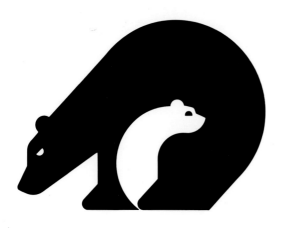

California Conservation Corps, State of California
Vanderbyl Design
Designers: Michael Vanderbyl,
Vanderbyl Design
San Francisco, USA

Shevlin Center
Commercial center
Vanderbyl Design
Designers: Michael Vanderbyl,
Vanderbyl Design
San Francisco, USA

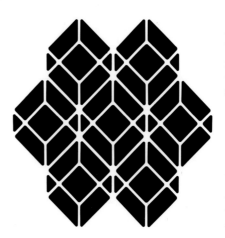

Community Action Team
Vanderbyl Design
Designers: Michael Vanderbyl,
Vanderbyl Design
San Francisco, USA

The Icehouse
Wholesale furniture complex
Vanderbyl Design
Designers: Michael Vanderbyl,
Vanderbyl Design
San Francisco, USA

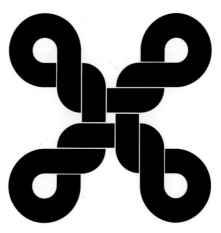

Met One
Windspeed indication equipment manufactuer
Vanderbyl Design
Designers: Michael Vanderbyl,
Vanderbyl Design
San Francisco, USA

Yachtmen's Exchange
Yachting equipment store
Vanderbyl Design
Designers: Michael Vanderbyl,
Vanderbyl Design
San Francisco, USA

Blum's

Confectionery
manufacturer
The Weller Institute
Designers: Dick Drayton,
Don Weller, Bob Maile
Los Angeles, USA

Blum's of San Francisco is
a company that makes and
sells fine candy. The
primary application of
their logotype is on
packaging. The logotype is
seldom used alone. It
usually is in the center of
a 'stained glass look' piece
of artwork that relates to
the specific packaging use
at hand. For example, on
the fruit cake can, it is
surrounded by stylized
fruit. The logotype itself is
always black but the
environment surrounding
it is usually colorful.

Bank of America Center, 555 California Street, San Francisco, California 94104. Telephone (415) 397-3077
A Subsidiary of Envirofood, Inc. an Affiliate of National Environment Corporation

1

2

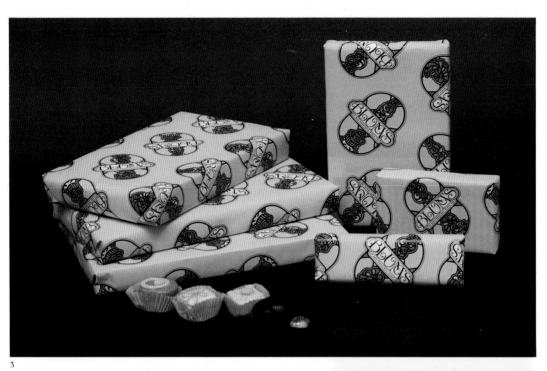

3

4

Lithographix Inc.
Printing firm
The Weller Institute
Designers: Don Weller,
Dennis Juett,
Dan Hanrahan
Los Angeles, USA

Lithographix Inc. is a fine
printing firm (offset
lithography) in Hollywood,
California. Although the
mark application is limited
to stationery and business
forms, it is well known to
designers and printing
buyers in the Los Angeles
area.

Wingtip
Courier service
Eisenberg Incorporated
Designer: Phil Waugh
Dallas, USA

WINGTIP

WINGTIP COURIERS WINGTIP COURIERS WINGTIP COURIERS WINGTIP COURIERS WINGTIP COURIERS

COURIERS

Eisenberg Chili
Eisenberg Incorporated
Designer: John March
Dallas, USA

WEBB&SONS
·INCORPORATED·

Webb & Sons
Printing preparation
service
Eisenberg Incorporated
Designer: Linda Eissler
Dallas, USA

Webb & Sons produces
fine quality four-color
offset separations and
black and white film
preparations, including
stripping and press
proofing for advertising
agencies, printers,
and major publications,
located in Dallas, Texas.

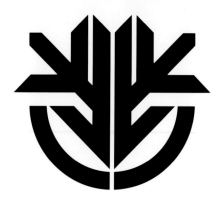

Missouri Botanical Garden
Hellmuth, Obata &
Kassabaum
Designer: Charles P. Reay
St. Louis, USA

The Missouri Botanical
Garden, one of the
premier horticultural
institutions of the world,
was established in 1859. Its
79 acres contain a
diversity of specimen
plants for viewing as well
as for research and
education.

1

Seiwa-En. The Japanese Garden

2   3

84

4

5

**Bank Administration
Institute**
James Lienhart Design
Designer: James Lienhart
Chicago, USA

BAI (Bank Administration
Institute) is an organization comprised of banks
across the United States.
BAI provides for its
member banks: periodic
conventions, seminars and
meetings; publications; a
central policy focus; public
relations and legislative
efforts — all geared toward
improving the banking on
a broad basis.

The new BAI trademark
was designed to symbolize
'Banking of the Future'.
The distinctive lower case
'b' is composed of two
elements which relate to
the concept that Bankers
are working together
through BAI to achieve a
level of banking
excellence. These
elements are designed
with an upward growth
motion and then placed
within a geometric shield
background. The visual
effect of graphic inter-
action is what growth
within the industry is all
about; the Banker and BAI
working together.

1

2

3

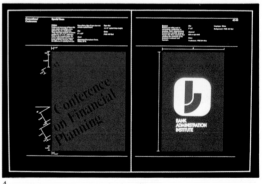

4

Heritage Bank
James Lienhart Design
Designer: James Lienhart
Chicago, USA

The Heritage Corporation owns a series of banks, all of which utilizes the Trademark and Heritage name as the basic elements to unify the identity.

The Trademark is based on the American Eagle which is directly connected to the word 'Heritage' as it is an American National symbol related to the American tradition. It is a strong and secure visual image developed as the bank's basic identity.

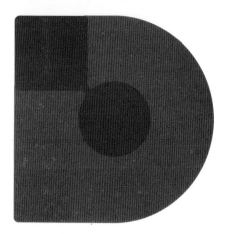

Darby Lithography
Printing company
James Lienhart Design
Designer: James Lienhart
Chicago, USA

Darby is a multi-faceted
printing/communications
company specializing in
offset printing, typesetting,
and audio/visual pro-
grams.

The 'D' trademark was
designed to always be
shown in two colors on all
material from stationery to
carpeting. The circle/
square within the 'D'
trademark is a
characterization of the dot
structure system in
printing. A total application, from printed forms to
transportation vehicles,
was implemented.

1

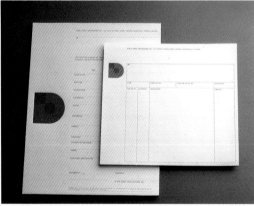

2

3

4

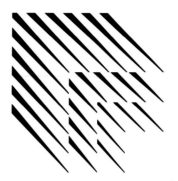

Point Northwest
Real estate development
Loucks Atelier
Designer: Jay Loucks,
C. Randall Sherman,
Paul Huber
Houston, USA

Loucks Atelier developed
this identity program for
Point Northwest, a 320
acre business/residential
land development. The
project is the first major
commitment in an other-
wise under promoted
and undeveloped area.
The logo is based on the
location, to help position
the project and increase
awareness of the area.
Applications include site
signage, vehicles, and
communication materials.

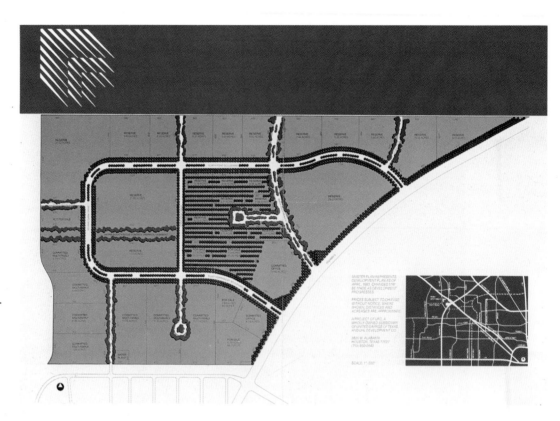

The Centre
Real estate development
Loucks Atelier
Designers: Jay Loucks,
C. Randall Sherman,
Paul Huber
Houston, USA

The Centre is a 74 acre,
multi use real estate
development, offering of-
fice and retail space,
hotels, pavilions, and
several support amenities.
The logo was applied to
building identification,
retail outlets, vehicles, site
signage and communica-
tion materials.

THE CENTRE

CENTRE ONE

THE CENTRE

1   2

Sea Wings
Charter service
Pirtle Design
Designer: Woody Pirtle
Dallas, USA

1

Cimarron Corporation
Livestock company
Pirtle Design
Designer: Woody Pirtle
Dallas, USA

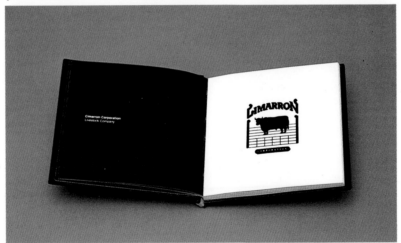

2

Dalts
Turn of the Century Bar
and Grill
Pirtle Design
Designer: Woody Pirtle
Dallas, USA

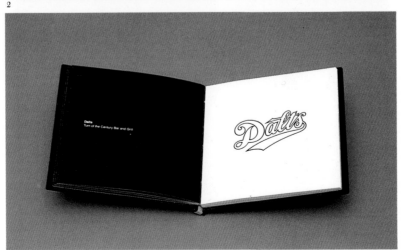

3

Summit Oilfield Corporation
Oilfield services company
Pirtle Design
Designer: Woody Pirtle
Dallas, USA

4

Zimmer Smith
Music production
company
Pirtle Design
Designer: Woody Pirtle
Dallas, USA

5

Sunny Produce
Florida citrus grower
Pirtle Design
Designer: Woody Pirtle
Dallas, USA

6

Heart Center
Clinic for cardiological
disorders
Pirtle Design
Designer: Woody Pirtle
Dallas, USA

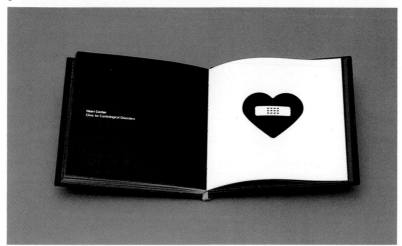

7

Architecture+

Architecture+
Architectural firm
Rodammer Morris
Associates
Designers: Kris
Rodammer,
Michael Morris, Hal Apple
Dallas, USA

1

2

3

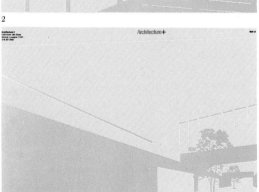

4

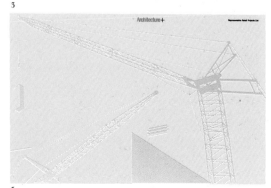

5

TDIndustries
An Employee Owned Company

TD Industries
Summerford Design Inc.
Designer: Jack
Summerford
Dallas, USA

This identity program was
implemented for TD
Industries, an employee-
owned company which is
engaged in heating,
air conditioning and
plumbing for major office
and apartment construc-
tion.

1

2

South Carolina National Bank
Anspach Grossman
Portugal Inc.
Designer: Eugene
Grossman
New York, USA

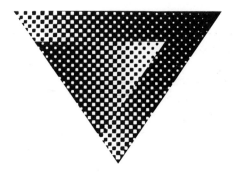

Swimaster
Recreational equipment
Anspach Grossman
Portugal Inc.
Designer: Eugene
Grossman
New York, USA

Richardson-Vicks
Health care products
Anspach Grossman
Portugal Inc.
Designers: Eugene
Grossman, Richard Felton,
Kristie Williams
New York, USA

Graswip
Product brand
identification
Anspach Grossman
Portugal Inc.
Designer: Eugene
Grossman
New York, USA

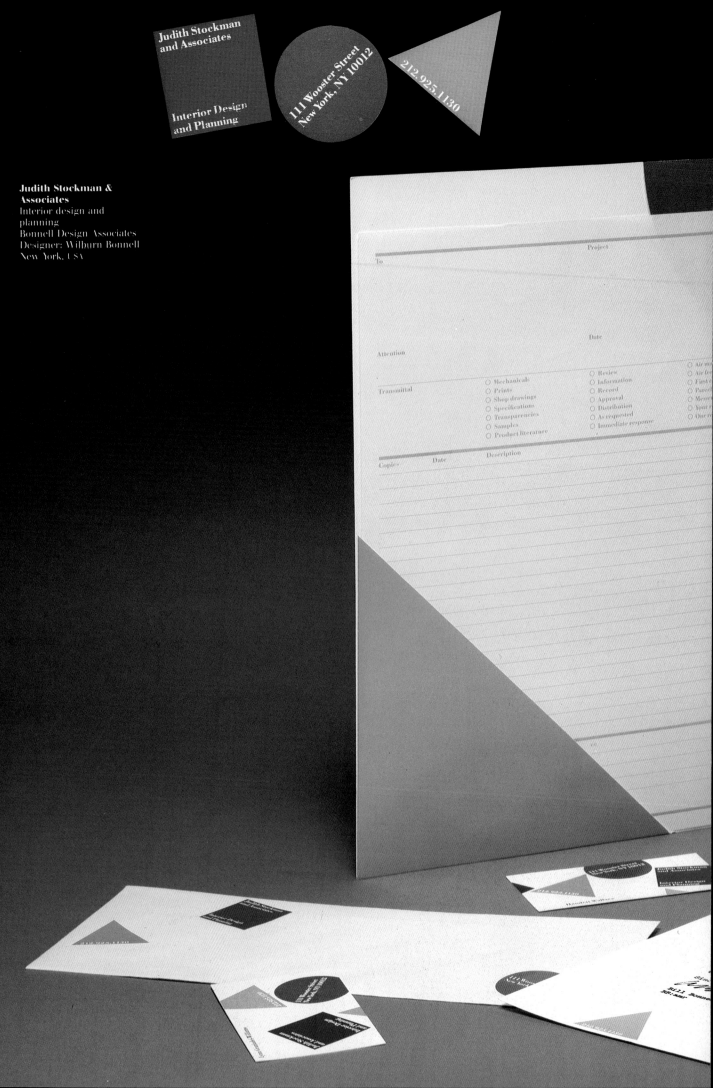

**Judith Stockman &
Associates**
Interior design and
planning
Bonnell Design Associates
Designer: Wilburn Bonnell
New York, USA

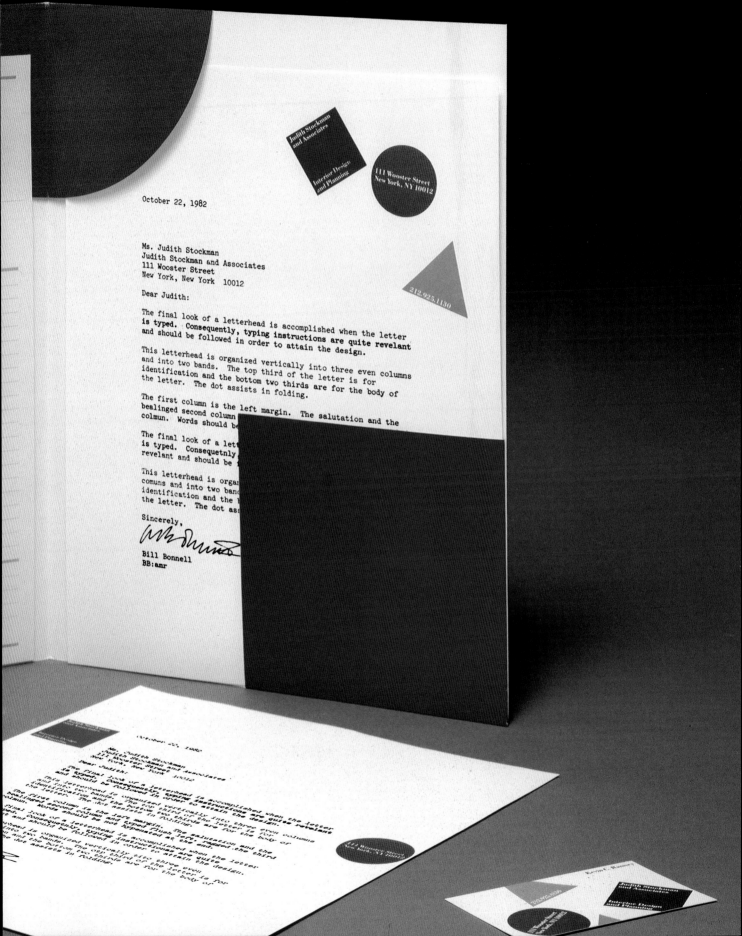

October 22, 1982

Ms. Judith Stockman
Judith Stockman and Associates
111 Wooster Street
New York, New York 10012

Dear Judith:

The final look of a letterhead is accomplished when the letter
is typed. Consequently, typing instructions are quite revelant
and should be followed in order to attain the design.

This letterhead is organized vertically into three even columns
and into two bands. The top third of the letter is for
identification and the bottom two thirds are for the body of
the letter. The dot assists in folding.

The first column is the left margin. The salutation and the
bealinged second column
colmun. Words should be

The final look of a lett
is typed. Consequetnly,
revelant and should be f

This letterhead is organ
comuns and into two band
identification and the b
the letter. The dot ass

Sincerely,

Bill Bonnell
BB:amr

Ryder Types
Advertising typographer
Bonnell Design Associates
Designer: Wilburn Bonnell
New York, USA

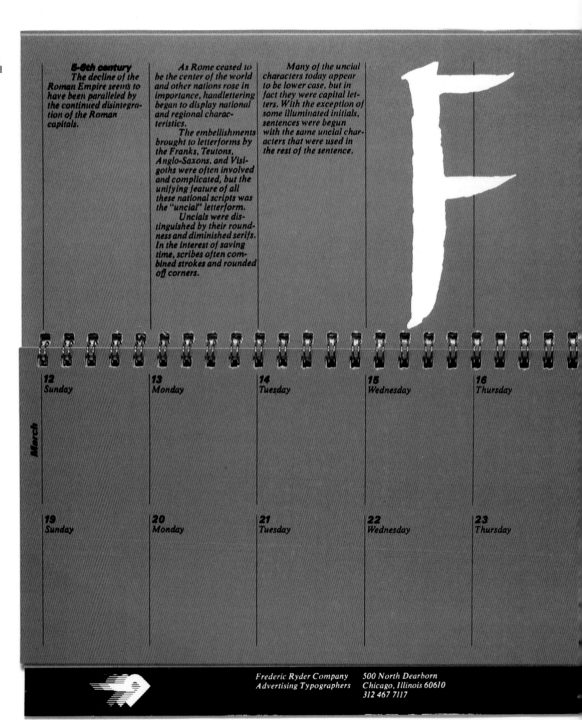

5-6th century
The decline of the Roman Empire seems to have been paralleled by the continued disintegration of the Roman capitals.

As Rome ceased to be the center of the world and other nations rose in importance, handlettering began to display national and regional characteristics.

The embellishments brought to letterforms by the Franks, Teutons, Anglo-Saxons, and Visigoths were often involved and complicated, but the unifying feature of all these national scripts was the "uncial" letterform.

Uncials were distinguished by their roundness and diminished serifs. In the interest of saving time, scribes often combined strokes and rounded off corners.

Many of the uncial characters today appear to be lower case, but in fact they were capital letters. With the exception of some illuminated initials, sentences were begun with the same uncial characters that were used in the rest of the sentence.

March

12 Sunday	**13** Monday	**14** Tuesday	**15** Wednesday	**16** Thursday
19 Sunday	**20** Monday	**21** Tuesday	**22** Wednesday	**23** Thursday

Frederic Ryder Company   500 North Dearborn
Advertising Typographers   Chicago, Illinois 60610
                            312 467 7117

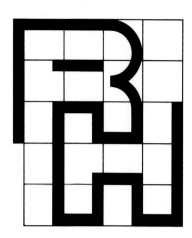

RH
RH development company.
Cook & Shanosky
Associates
Designers: Roger Cook,
Don Shanosky
Princeton, New Jersey, USA

**The Johnson
Companies**
Financial and planning
services
Cook & Shanosky
Associates
Designers: Roger Cook,
Don Shanosky
Princeton, New Jersey, USA

Ciba Services
Ciba Geigy
Pharmaceuticals
Cook & Shanosky
Associates
Designers: Roger Cook,
Don Shanosky
Princeton, New Jersey, USA

This symbol was devel-
oped for Ciba Services, a
division of Ciba-Geigy
Pharmaceuticals, which
offers educational and
research information and
literature to medical
professionals.

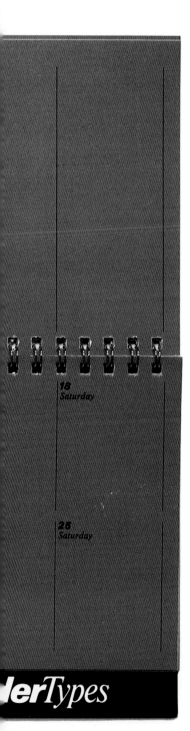

_ler_Types

CTE
Christian Theological
Education of the United
Presbyterian Church, USA
Cook & Shanosky
Associates
Designers: Roger Cook,
Don Shanosky
Princeton, New Jersey, USA

Symbol Signs
Cook & Shanosky
Associates
Designers: Roger Cook,
Don Shanosky
Princeton, New Jersey, USA

This AIGA poster shows the first 34 symbols designed by Cook & Shanosky for the United States Department of Transportation as part of their sign program.

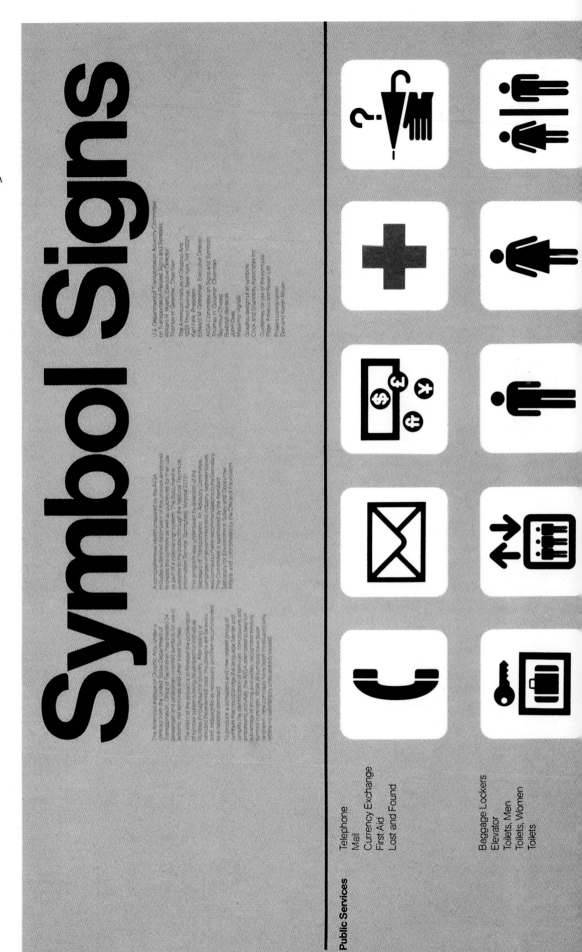

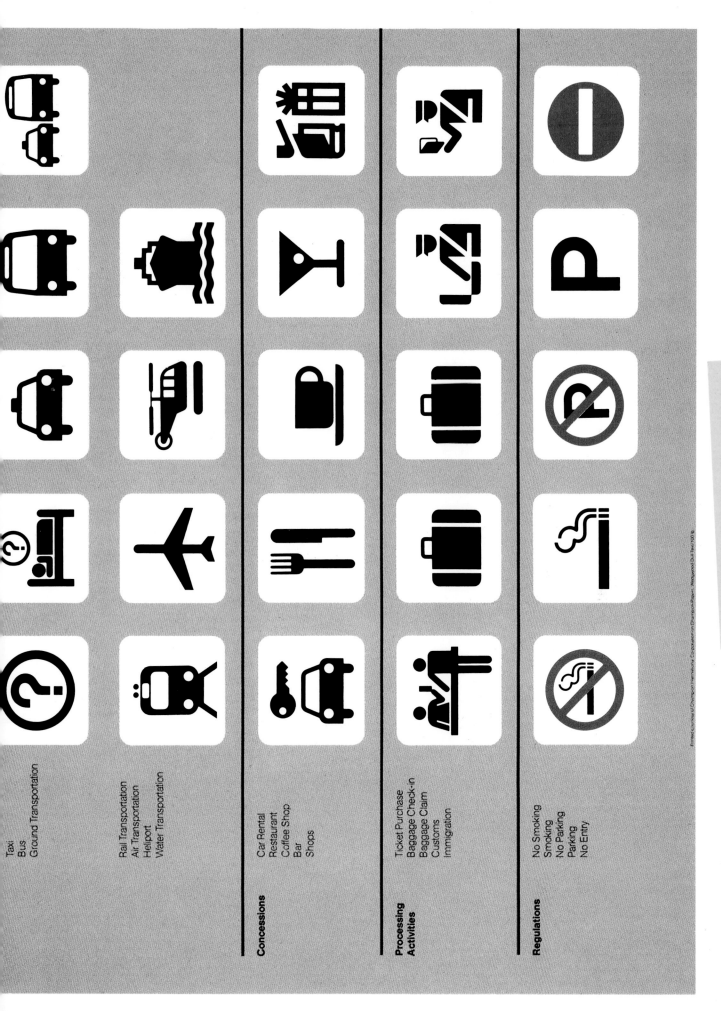

Taxi
Bus
Ground Transportation

Rail Transportation
Air Transportation
Heliport
Water Transportation

Concessions

Car Rental
Restaurant
Coffee Shop
Bar
Shops

**Processing
Activities**

Ticket Purchase
Baggage Check-in
Baggage Claim
Customs
Immigration

Regulations

No Smoking
Smoking
No Parking
Parking
No Entry

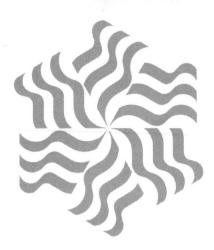

United Nations Plaza Hotel
Rudolph de Harak & Associates
Designer: Rudolph de Harak
New York, USA

UNITED
NATIONS
PLAZA
HOTEL

One United Nations Plaza
New York, New York 10017
Telephone 212 355-3400

Helmut A. Horn
General Manager

Managed by Hyatt International Corporation

THE
INFORMATION
BANK

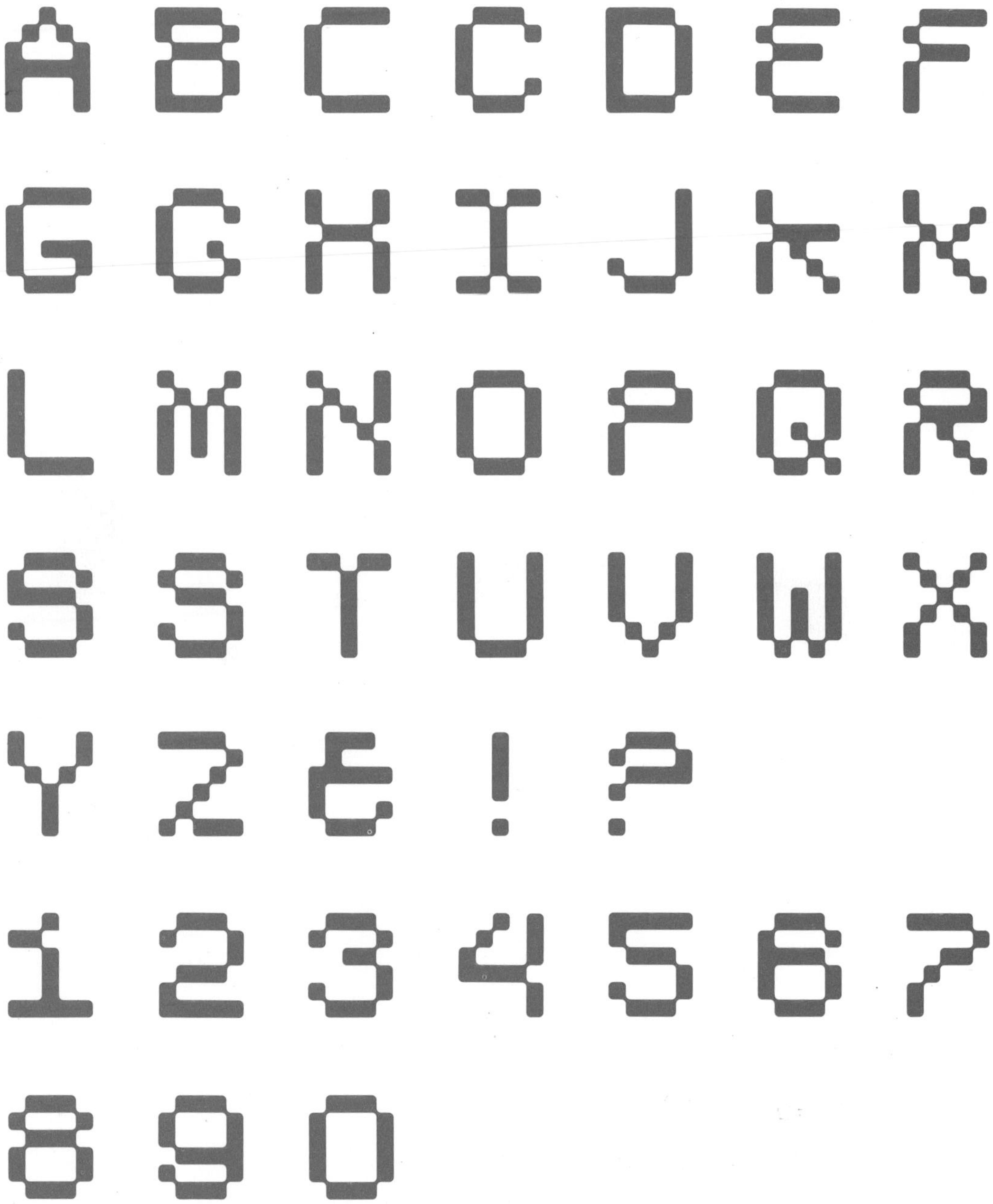

A B C C D E F

The Information Bank
Rudolph de Harak &
Associates
Designer: Rudolph de
Harak
New York, USA

G G H I J K K

L M N O P Q R

S S T U V W X

Y Z E ! ?

1 2 3 4 5 6 7

8 9 0

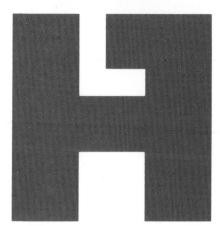

Horizon
Lighting company
Rudolph de Harak &
Associates
Designer: Rudolph de
Harak
New York, USA

Horizon Lighting

Horizon Lighting Company   50 Charles Street   Westwood. New Jersey 07675

Kurt Versen
Incandescent and mercury
lighting
Rudolph de Harak &
Associates
Designer: Rudolph de
Harak
New York, USA

Symboisis
Filmmakers
Rudolph de Harak &
Associates
Designer: Rudolph de
Harak
New York, USA

Oyster Bar & Restaurant
Rudolph de Harak &
Associates
Designer: Rudolph de
Harak
New York, USA

I Love New York
New York City promotion
Milton Glaser Inc.
Designer: Milton Glaser
New York, USA

Windows on the world
Restaurant
Milton Glaser Inc.
Designer: Milton Glaser
New York, USA

CTW
Children's Television
Workshop
Milton Glaser Inc.
Designer: Milton Glaser
New York, USA

Barron's
Publisher
Milton Glaser Inc.
Designer: Milton Glaser
New York, USA

Spa Cafe
Restaurant/Cafe
Milton Glaser Inc.
Designer: Milton Glaser
New York, USA

The Celler in the Sky
Restaurant
Milton Glaser Inc.
Designer: Milton Glaser
New York, USA

Jennie's Cookery
Restaurant
Milton Glaser Inc.
Designer: Milton Glaser
New York, USA

American Restaurant
Milton Glaser Inc.
Designer: Milton Glaser
New York, USA

Barbizon
Modeling Agency
Milton Glaser Inc.
Designer: Milton Glaser
New York, USA

East Sixty-Third Street at Lexington Avenue New York, New York 10021 (212) 838-5700 (800) 223-1020 Telex 220060

The Great House
Restaurant
Milton Glaser Inc.
Designer: Milton Glaser
New York, USA

Pizza Piazza
Restaurant
Milton Glaser Inc.
Designer: Milton Glas
New York, USA

PIZZAPIAZZA

...arge shrimp, white radish salad / 6.75
...egetable paté, plum tomato sauce / 4.75
...rapped in smoked salmon, vinaigrette / 5.95
...or oysters, iced or roasted on rock salt / 5.75
...eafood sausage, lobster sauce / 4.75
...ttes of ginger-marinated chicken / 4.75
...ushrooms & onions on brioche toast / 4.75
...consommé with chicken dumplings / 2.75
...sh chowder with spring vegetables / 2.75

...NNER SPECIALTIES

...on filled with a mousse of scallops / 18.50
...louse tureen of Florida seafood / 19.50
...sea bass for two, served with its broth / 32.50
...e of red snapper, basil butter sauce / 16.50
...poached, grilled or pan-fried / market price
...oasted crisp, spiced new cabbage / 13.50
...red with two vinegars, glazed pears & cream / 13.50
...f veal with citrus fruits & avocado / 18.50
...lamb, gratin of eggplant & tomato / 18.50
...zed onions, sweet red peppers & rosemary / 18.25

...ED OVER CHARCOAL

...ed potatoes—lemon, herb, anchovy or other butters

...t mignon / 18.75, Double lamb chops / 19.50
...ard of beef or veal / 18.00, Swordfish steak / 16.50
...getable Basket / priced per choice

...d with red onion, black olives & cumin dressing / 3.75
...l of local & unusual greens / 3.50

...with wine sapphire cream, raspberry syrup / 3.75
...amel flan with brandied oranges / 3.25
...reams & sorbets are made here / 2.50

...louse Sideboard offers new selections daily.

...owers Of Quayside / Miami, Florida

785 BROADWAY   NEW YORK, N.Y. 10003

RBSD

RBS+D
Architectural firm
Gottschalk + Ash
International
Designers: Ken Carbone,
Leslie Smolan,
Steve Orant
New York, USA

This logo was developed
for the architectural firm
of Rogers, Burgun,
Shahine, and Deschler,
specializing in the design
of hospitals and health
care facilities.

1

2

★ARRIVE★

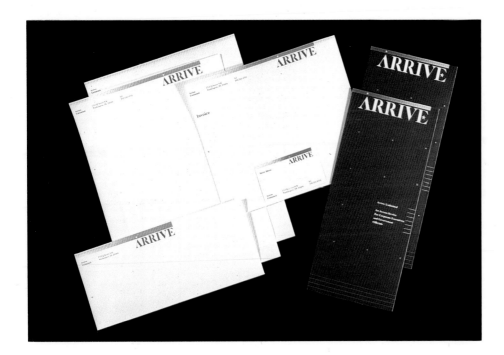

Arrive
Public relations firm
Gottschalk + Ash
International
Designers: Leslie Smolan,
Steve Orant
New York, USA

Arrive is a public relations
firm located in Washington,
DC, that specializes in the
coordination and
management of political
events and state visits.

The Eye Institute
Eye care clinic
Gottschalk + Ash
International
Designers: Ken Carbone,
Leslie Smolan
New York, USA

This symbol was developed
for the Eye Institute, an eye
clinic in Philadelphia,
Pennsylvania. The halftone
translation of the outer
'E' characterizes the 'fuzzy'
or blurred quality of
impaired vision, while the
inner 'E' is clear and
precise, symbolizing a
vision problem that has
been corrected.

1

Flatbush Ave.
Urban revitalization
program
Gottschalk + Ash
International
Designers: Leslie Smolan,
Ken Carbone
New York, USA

Flatbush Ave. is an urban
revitalization campaign for
Brooklyn, New York. The
variations on the basic
logotype were used for
several different applications which include sales
promotion identifications,
signage, and newsletter
mastheads.
1. Logotype for main/
   commercial/retail strip
2. Community newsletter
   masthead
3. Sales promotion
   identification
4. Sales promotion
   identification

F L A S H

2

5

6

3

Sale Days

Sales Days

4

German American Chamber of Commerce
Willi Kunz Associates
Designer: Willi Kunz
New York, USA

The key element of an identity program for the German American Chamber of Commerce is a symbol based on the merger of the German and American flags within a global shape. It is printed in green in conjunction with a consistent typographic nomenclature in gray. To achieve unity, the program includes all communications materials such as stationery, labels, forms and newsletters in German and English. As a cover design for all publications, a four-color version of the symbol was developed in black, red, yellow, and blue; a combination of the colors of both nations.

1

2

Merit
Gasoline company
Willi Kunz Associates
Designers: Willi Kunz,
Eugene Grossman
New York, USA

This symbol, related to the
letterform 'M', serves as
the main identifier in a
total identification
program which includes
oil cans, gasoline pumps,
uniforms, and promotional
materials for the Merit
Gasoline stations.

This sign consists of a
three dimensional version
of the symbol, cantilevered
above a vertical beam in
black enamel, containing
the illuminated Merit
logotype.

1

2

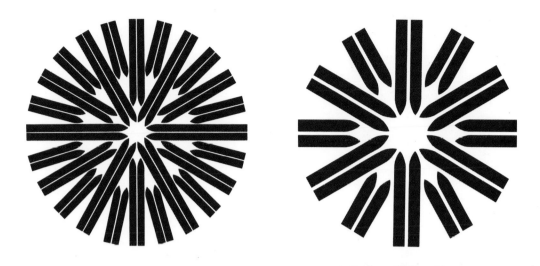

United States Deaf Skiers Association 3rd Biennial National Convention

February 27– March 4, 1972

North Conway, New Hampshire

DESIGNED BY DAVID LEIGH TRADEMARK OF THE UNITED STATES DEAF SKIERS ASSOCIATION

**United States Deaf
Skiers Association**
David Leigh
Designer: David Leigh
New York, USA

The objective of the corporate identity program for the United States Deaf Skiers Association was to create a memorable symbol for the deaf skiers and to impart the seriousness and dignity of the group. The problem consisted of the need to create a symbol easily adaptable for a wide variety of applications ranging from posters to letterheads to tiny tack pins. the solution was 'Skimark', which shows skis of three sizes converging into a center, illustrating the unity of skiers.

Madison East Coiffures
Jonson, Pedersen, Hinrichs
& Shakery Inc.
Designer: B. Martin
Pedersen
New York, USA

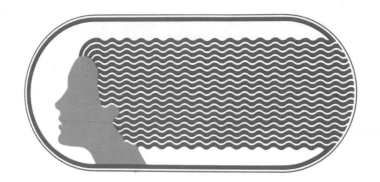

**Scandinavia Travel
Bureau**
Travel agency
Jonson, Pedersen, Hinrichs
& Shakery Inc.
Designer: B. Martin
Pedersen
New York, USA

WNYC
Public radio station
Pentagram
Designers: Colin Forbes,
Dan Friedman
New York, USA

This corporate identity for
New York's own public
service radio station was
developed by Pentagram in
1981. In the new logo, the
last three letters of the
name are emphasized to
highlight the station's
location.

AM83   FM94   TV31

1

2

JHANEBARNES

1

2

3

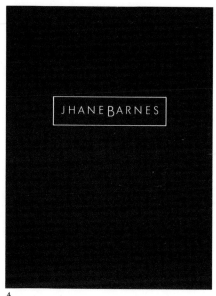

4

Jhane Barnes
Fashion designer
Pentagram
Designers: Dan Friedman,
Colin Forbes
New York, USA

An identity program was
developed by Pentagram for
Jhane Barnes, a fashion designer, using visual
metaphors for fabric,
sewing, cutting, dyeing and
labels.

American Savings Bank
Pushpin Lubalin Peckolick
Designers: Alan Peckolick,
Tony DiSpigna
New York, USA

Antonovich
Pushpin Lubalin Peckolick
Designers: Alan Peckolick,
Tony DiSpigna
New York, USA

Antonovich

CBS Video
Pushpin Lubalin Peckolick
Designers: Alan Peckolick,
Tony DiSpigna
New York, USA

Food and Wine
Magazine
Pushpin Lubalin Peckolick
Designers: Jessica Weber,
Alan Peckolick,
Tony DiSpigna
New York, USA

FOOD&WINE

Helena Rubenstein
Cosmetics company.
Pushpin Lubalin Peckolick
Designers: Alan Peckolick,
Tom Carnase
New York, USA

**Pushpin Lubalin
Peckolick**
Design company
Designers: Seymour
Chwast
Alan Peckolick
New York, USA

U&lc.

AaBbCcDdEeFfGgHhIiJjKkLlMmNnOoPp   QqRrSsTtUuVvWwXxYyZz1234567890&ÆŒ$¢£%!?()[]

U&LC
Upper and Lower Case
magazine
Pushpin Lubalin Peckolick
Designers: Herb Lubalin,
Tom Carnase
New York, USA

Families

Families
Magazine
Pushpin Lubalin Peckolick
Designers: Herb Lubalin,
Michael Aron
New York, USA

Time-Life
Publisher
Arnold Saks Inc.
Designer: Arnold Saks
New York, USA

This is a proposed logo for
Time-Life Inc., a publisher
of books and magazines
in the United States.

TIME INCORPORATED

NEED
Near East Emergency
Donations
Arnold Saks Inc.
Designer: Arnold Saks
New York, USA

**New York State Urban
Development
Corporation**
State agency for
development programs
Arnold Saks Inc.
Designer: Arnold Saks
New York, USA

InProp
Real estate investment trust
Arnold Saks Inc.
Designer: Arnold Saks
New York, USA

Laverne

Laverne
Furniture and wall
coverings
Arnold Saks Inc.
Designer: Arnold Saks
New York, USA

Museum Mile

Museum Mile
Museum guide
Arnold Saks Inc.
Designer: Arnold Saks
New York, USA

Transnitro
Importer of nitrogen
Arnold Saks Inc.
Designer: Arnold Saks
New York, USA

Eastex
Paper and packaging
company
Arnold Saks Inc.
Designer: Arnold Saks
New York, USA

TRW

TRW
Manufacturing
conglomerate
Siegel & Gale
Designers: Don Ervin,
Debbie Osteen
New York, USA

TRW is a $5 billion
manufacturing conglomer-
ate specializing in high-
technology products and
services for the automo-
tive, defense, space, and
energy industries. Its
products range from seat
belt reels to communi-
cations satellites, from
drill bits to missile control
systems, from airplane
propellors to video game
parts. TRW's international
headquarters are in
Cleveland, Ohio.

1

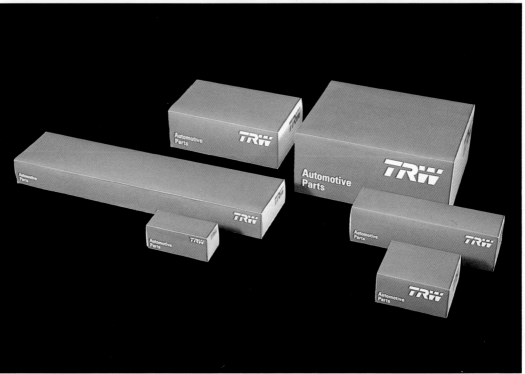

2

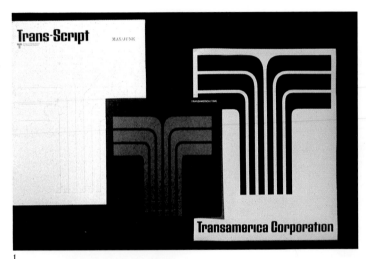

Transamerica
Siegel & Gale
Designer: Don Ervin
New York, USA

2

1

Mellon Bank
Siegel & Gale
Designer: Don
New York, USA

1

2

GRACE

WR Grace & Co.
Chemical and natural
resource company.
George Tscherny Inc.
Designers: George
Tscherny, Helen Curry,
Sandra Wheat,
Elizabeth Coburn Ball
New York, USA

WRGrace & Co., founded
127 years ago, is today an
international company
worldwide interests in
chemicals, natural
resources, and selected
consumer services.

George Tscherny Inc.,
began work on the Grace
corporate identification
program in 1973. Applica-
tions include the design
manual, annual reports,
printed promotional
material, signage, and
vehicle and product
identification.

1

2

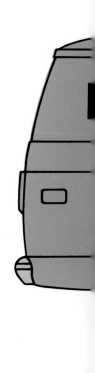

5

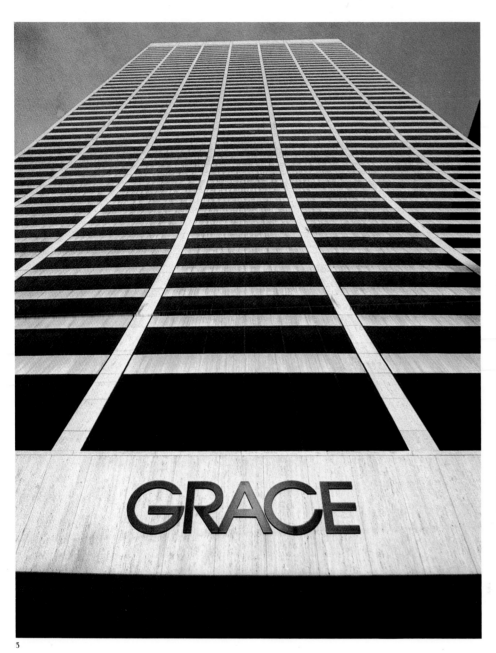

3

Graphics Standards/ Free Standing Signs

4

6

Sesame Street
Children's educational
magazine
Henry Wolf Productions Inc.
Designer: Henry Wolf
New York, USA

Offshore Power Systems
Vignelli Associates
Designer: Massimo Vignelli
New York, USA

Lutheran Church in America
1976 Convention graphics
Vignelli Associates
Designer: Massimo Vignelli
New York, USA

St. Peter's Church
Vignelli Associates
Designers: Massimo
Vignelli, Henry Alchek
New York, USA

Santa Cruz
Apparel design and
manufacturer
Vignelli Associates
Designers: Massimo
Vignelli, Michael Bierut
New York, USA

1

3

2

3

SantaCruz

SantaCruz

SantaCruz

Santa Cruz
180 Utah Avenue, South San Francisco, California 94080
Telephone (415) 873-4815, Telex 510 371 7410

4

Santa Cruz
180 Utah Avenue, South San Francisco, California 94080
Telephone (415) 873-4815, Telex 510 371 7410

5

Santa Cruz
180 Utah Avenue, South San Francisco, California 94080
Telephone (415) 873-4815, Telex 510 371 7410

6

SantaCruz

SantaCruz

SantaCruz

Santa Cruz
180 Utah Avenue, South San Francisco, California 94080
Telephone (415) 873-4815, Telex 510 371 7410

7

Santa Cruz
180 Utah Avenue, South San Francisco, California 94080
Telephone (415) 873-4815, Telex 510 371 7410

8

Santa Cruz
180 Utah Avenue, South San Francisco, California 94080
Telephone (415) 873-4815, Telex 510 371 7410

9

Chapter II

South America

Argentina

Brazil

City of Buenos Aires
Identification system
Arq. González Ruiz and
Associates
Designers: Guillermo
González Ruiz,
Ronald Shakespear,
Eduardo Canovas
Buenos Aires, Argentina

1

2

3

Municipalidad de
la Ciudad de
Buenos Aires

4

5

Vinilia
Vinyl paper manufacturer
Arq. González Ruiz and
Associates
Designer: Guillermo
Gonzáles Ruiz
Buenos Aires, Argentina

The identification system
for Vinilia was developed
in 1977 by Arq. González
Ruiz and Associates of
Buenos Aires, Argentina.
The applications for
Vinilia, a vinyl paper
manufacturer, include
packaging, calendars,
catalogues, magazine
design, and other
promotional materials.

1

2

Austral
Private Argentinian airline
Arq. González Ruiz and
Associates
Designer: Guillermo
González Ruiz
Buenos Aires, Argentina

2

1

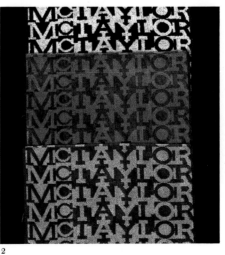

McTaylor
Mode for men
Arq. González Ruiz and
Associates
Designer: Guillermo
González Ruiz
Buenos Aires, Argentina

1

2

135

Banco de Galicia
Bank of Galicia
Arq. González Ruiz and
Associates
Designer: Guillermo
González Ruiz
Buenos Aires, Argentina

1

2

3

banespa

Banespa
Brazilian bank
Cauduro/Martino
Arquitetos Associados
Designers: João Carlos
Cauduro, Ludovico A.
Martino, Marco A. A.
Rezende
São Paulo, Brazil

Banespa is one of the
largest banks in Brazil
with over 16,000
employees and 300
branches. Their corporate
identity program was
designed from 1974–78
and launched in 1976 to
create a new image for the
bank.

1

2

3

4

auxiliar

Auxiliar

Brazilian bank
Cauduro/Martino Arquitetos
Associados
Designers: João Carlos
Cauduro, Ludovico A.
Martino, Marco A. A.
Rezende
São Paulo, Brazil

The corporate identity
program for Auxiliar, a
private Brazilian bank, was
implemented in 1978, when
they decided to renew their
traditional image and
promote a new profile; that
of a warm-hearted,
human and modern bank.

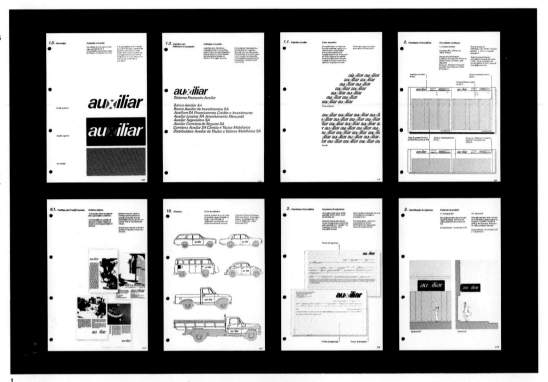

1

CESP

CESP

São Paulo State Electrical
Authority
Cauduro/Martino Arquitetos
Associados
Designers: João Carlos
Cauduro, Ludovico A.
Martino, Marco A. A.
Rezende
São Paulo, Brazil

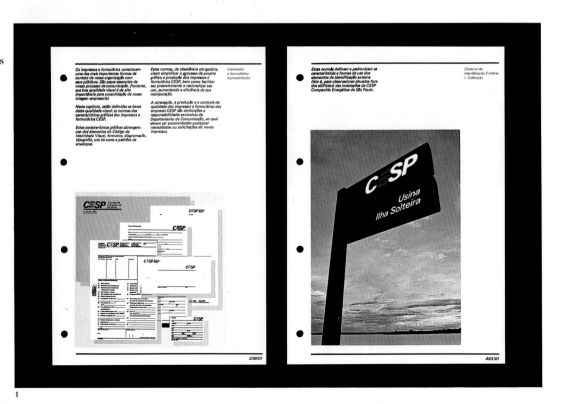

1

FRANKI

Franki
Engineering firm
Joaquim Redig
Designer: Joaquim Redig
Rio de Janeiro, Brazil

1

2

MALASARTES

Malasartes
Children's bookshop
Joaquim Redig
Designers: Joaquim Redig,
Suzana Fonseca
Rio de Janeiro, Brazil

E   M

A   S

Lá na Gávea tem uma rua

Nessa rua tem um Shopping

M   Nesse shopping tem quatro Andares

No Terceiro tem um corredor   A

Nesse corredor tem uma Loja

Nessa loja tem Estantes

S   Nessas estantes tem Muitos livros

Nesses Livros tem histórias   T

Nessas histórias tem um Mundo

A   para você se divertir

R

R   Venha descobrir e curtir   S

A

Livraria   L

MALASARTES

E   Brinquedos e Papéis

Rua M. de São Vicente 52 loja 367 Rio

M

E

A

M

$\mathbb{S}$

A

$\mathbb{S}$

A

?

Lá na Gávea tem uma rua
Nessa rua tem um $\mathbb{S}$hopping
Nesse shopping tem quatro **A**ndares
No **T**erceiro tem um corredor
Nesse corredor tem uma **L**oja
Nessa loja tem **E**stantes
Nessas estantes tem **M**uitos livros
Nesses **L**ivros tem histórias
Nessas histórias tem um **M**undo
para você se divertir

T

R

S

Venha descobrir e curtir

A

L

Livraria

MALASARTES

E

Brinquedos e Papéis

Rua M. de São Vicente 52 loja 367 Rio

FURNAS

Furnas
Power company
Joaquim Redig
Designer: Joaquim Redig
Rio de Janeiro, Brazil

Furnas Centrais Elétricas'
old symbol was
represented by a realistic
drawing of a transmission
tower. The new symbol
intends to communicate
the same idea, but
simplified. This program
was one of the first
complete corporate
identity systems consisten-
ly applied in Brazil, and
therefore considered a
pioneer project.

1

2

3

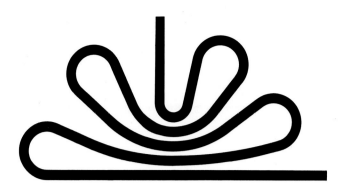

NOVA AMÉRICA

...oduzimos 6
...s e meio por mês.
...sim, não é difícil
...uem é a maior
...ia têxtil do país.
...apital brasileiro,
...istração brasileira
...de obra
...ira, tudo o que
...nos fica no Brasil.
...ve os 8 milhões
...de dólares que
...nos em exportações
... passado.
...ossos tecidos
...mundo, vestindo
...cendo as pessoas
...egantes.
...oduzimos também
...on, o revestimento
...que mais
...faz no mercado,
...uindo com muita
... economia os
...onais tacos de madeira.
Tudo isto é a fortuna
que vamos tecendo
dia-a-dia, com nossos 7 mil
operários e técnicos.
São fortunas como
esta que tornam um país
mais rico e um povo
mais desenvolvido.

NOVA AMÉRICA

1

Nova América
Textile company
Joaquim Redig
Designer: Joaquim Redig
Rio de Janeiro, Brazil

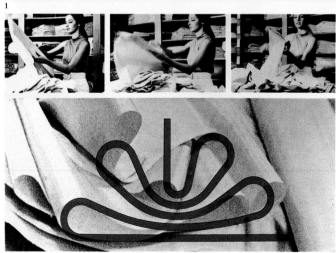

2

143

Caixa
State bank
Joaquim Redig
Designers: Joaquim Redig,
Rita Horta
Rio de Janeiro, Brazil

Caixa Económica Federal
is the state bank whose
services are used widely
and has been known
popularly as 'Caixa' for
many decades. 'Caixa'
meaning box, evokes a
place to keep money. The
new graphic identity
program emphasizes their
traditional verbal identity
and relates to the concept
of the box.

1

2

3

4

5

6

7

8

9

Sumaré

Sumaré
DICV Designo Ltd.
Designer: Alexandre
Wollner
São Paulo, Brazil

Sumaré Industrias
Químicas is a manufac-
turer of protective coatings
for offshore industries
and equipment, located in
São Paulo, Brazil.

1

2

146

1

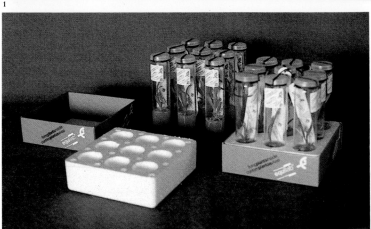

2

Equilab
Genetic plant improvement
laboratory
DICV Designo Ltd.
Designer: Alexandre
Wollner
São Paulo, Brazil

Chapter III

Asia

Hong Kong
India
Israel
Japan
Korea
Turkey

Dah Sing Bank
Hong Kong bank
Graphic Communication
Ltd.
Designer: Henry Steiner
Hong Kong

大新銀行

DahSingBank

大新銀行

1

Dah Sing Bank, Ltd

World-Wide House, 19 Des Voeux Road Central, Hong Kong

telephone: 5-243126 cable: Dahsingbank telex: 74063 DBB HK

2

CHEQUE BOOK   支票簿

A/C NO   賬號

A/C NAME   戶名

PLEASE KEEP THIS
CHEQUE BOOK
UNDER LOCK AND KEY
此支票簿請領妥收藏

3

DahSingBank 大新銀行

AL 435076   AL 435100

DahSingBank 大新銀行

SAVINGS ACCOUNT PASSBOOK 活期儲蓄存摺

4

151

I Club
Private club
Graphic Communication
Ltd.
Designer: Henry Steiner
Hong Kong

The I Club is a private
dining club in Hong Kong.
Their corporate identity is
built on not just one form
of the letter 'I', but on
many variations.

1

2

5

6

3

A PRIVATE CLUB.
AN INTERNATIONAL LIFESTYLE.
5·218131
OPENING THIS SUMMER.

A PRIVATE CLUB.
AN INTERNATIONAL LIFESTYLE.
5·218131
OPENING THIS SUMMER.

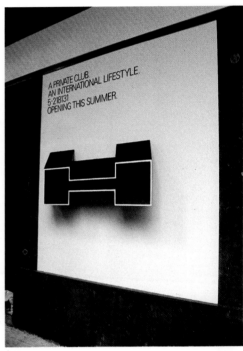

4

A PRIVATE CLUB.
AN INTERNATIONAL LIFESTYLE.
5·218131
OPENING THIS SUMMER.

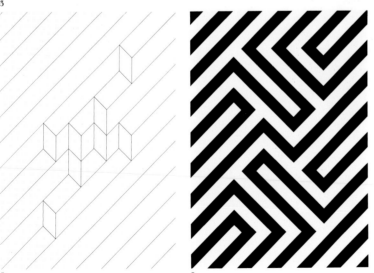

7

8

9

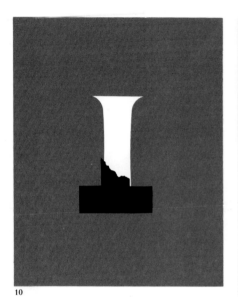

10

Hong Kong with its energy, drive and restless movement is often compared with New York — without the culture. In the visual arts in particular, Hong Kong has needed a centre where contemporary painting, sculpture, furniture and interior design of international calibre could be enjoyed as integral parts of a complete, planned environment.

Alfred Siu, managing director of OLS Holdings Ltd. recognised this need and conceived I as a private club in which members could meet at The Collection, dine in the restaurants or exercise in the Health Spa in an environment which is an art gallery designed for entertainment.

Art and design have been the inspiration for I. Whether it be painting, sculpture or furniture, art is an essential part of walking through spaces designed to flow from one area to the next.

New York designer, Joe D'Urso, created the setting for all Club activities. With areas defined by curving or straight walls, accented by pillars in contrasting shapes, he and Alfred Siu chose each piece of furniture, each plate, each glass, not only to suit its function but to relate in form, colour and texture to the whole environment.

I, in the podium, Bank of America Tower, commands a total space of 58,000 sq.ft. on the ground, first and second floors. The 3rd floor is reserved for 100 covered parking spaces. With the largest area of indoor space of any club in Central, I presents to its members an international lifestyle in a club so planned that, whether eating, exercising or simply passing from one part of the interior to another, there is always something of interest to see, something to stimulate the imagination.

Headed by master chefs, the Club's Chinese and Western restaurants will entice members seeking the finest cuisine in beautiful surroundings, away from the noisy crush of Central's overcrowded public places. Private functions, too, will be hosted in rooms where the furniture is as much a part of the whole experience of dining as the food itself.

Le Corbusier, Mackintosh, Mies Van der Rohe, the vanguard of 20th century avant garde architecture, captured their vision of design in sculptural furniture. Each of these men, and Bellini and Josef Hoffman, too, has a room devoted to his work where, in elegant and attentive surroundings, members and their guests can experience for themselves design as art.

I pm, the Club's own nightclub, will turn its spotlight on top international performers, invited to Hong Kong to carry I's entertainment into the night.

In a club which is planned as an art environment there must be an art gallery. I has not one gallery, but two. The first houses the personal collection of Alfred Siu, on loan to the Club. The other will be the venue for special exhibitions.

For the grand opening, Andy Warhol will come in person, bringing to I a collection of his work, paintings and prints, which have never been seen before in Hong Kong.

But this is only the beginning of the excitement that I will create in Hong Kong.

In exhibitions of jewellery, prints, sculptures, fashions and every kind of live entertainment, I will be a Hong Kong centre for the best the world can offer.

Everything in I has been designed to stimulate.

ALL ITEMS ILLUSTRATED IN THIS BROCHURE HAVE BEEN ORDERED AND WILL BE USED IN THE CLUB.

11

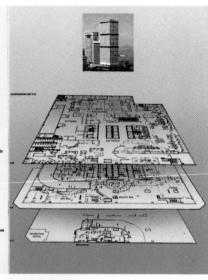

12

14

The Library

Over 100 different periodicals, the acknowledged leaders in art, architecture and design, fashion and photography, sport, travel and music will join the books on the library shelves each month.

Immediately adjacent is the library theatre which will screen the most important films from around the world and the best of the English language features. Film classics will be shown regularly.

15

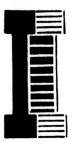 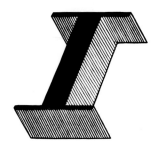 

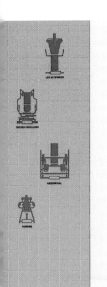

LEG EXTENSION

DOUBLE SHOULDER

ABDOMINAL

ROWING

The Spa

The Spa is a centre for mind and body where the equipment, by Nautilus, has been so designed that, under the guidance of the Club's own instructor, members can plan a fitness programme tailored to their own individual needs.

A Le Corbusier 'chaise lounge', which is shown in New York's Museum of Modern Art as an example of the French architect's finest work, is just one of the furnishings in the men's health area.

In the women's section, 'Wink' a chair in brilliant colours by Toshiyuki Kita gives a feeling of cheerful comfort.

The Spa encompasses the health food Spa Bar, the saunas, and jacuzzi. The California hot tub can be booked for private parties.

Dance and yoga classes are just two of the other activities planned for the Spa.

The I Lounge

This is the Club's focal point for the cocktail hour. The I Lounge is designed as an active and elegant meeting place for all hours.

Whether the mood is for intimate conversation, simply a nightcap or the relaxation provided by the piano's unobtrusive background, the I Lounge caters for all I's members and their guests.

The lounge will also be the centre for wine tastings, bringing vintages from the established vineyards of Europe and offering the opportunity to savour the popular wines of California and Australia.

13

...its the Art
...g map for

..., will bring a
...e opening

...and then —
...ogue in the
...rought to
...I.

The Restaurant

Master Chefs will bring to I imaginative cuisine for all palates in an atmosphere which continues the prevailing theme of art.

Western and Chinese cuisine, using the freshest local and imported foods will make for a truly international bill of fare.

Through the restaurant runs a 10 ft. wide passageway leading from the Art Forum to the private function rooms. Sculpture, exhibitions of jewellery or ceramics are envisaged for this space, which can be seen from all parts of the restaurant.

Accompanied by the finest wines and spirits, special festivals will feature foods with a national or regional theme.

16

Swedish Motors

Swedish Motors
Automobile distributor
Graphic Communication
Ltd.
Designer: Henry Steiner
Hong Kong

1

2

3

4

5

Hindustan Petroleum
Petroleum corporation
Graphic Communication
Concepts
Designers: Sudarshan
Dheer, Shashis
Bombay, India

1

2

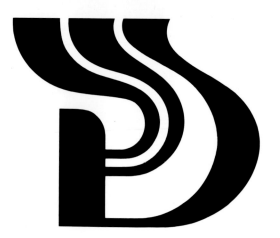

PD Kothari & Co.
Diamond exporter
Graphic Communication
Concepts
Designers: Sudarshan
Dheer, Pravin Panchal,
Narendra Vaidya,
Neclkamal Patil
Bombay, India

1

2

3

**Mahavir Refractories
Pvt. Ltd.**
Fire brick manufacturer
Graphic Communication
Concepts
Designers: Sudarshan
Dheer, Suresh Chinchinrar
Bombay, India

1

2

3

Kissan
Food processor
Graphic Communication
Concepts
Designers: Sudarshan
Dheer, Calistus Pereira
Bombay, India

1

2

Eco
Chemical products
manufacturer
Dan Reisinger Designs
Designer: Dan Reisinger
Tel Aviv, Israel

Iscar
Hardmetal industrial
products
Dan Reisinger Designs
Designer: Dan Reisinger
Tel Aviv, Israel

ISCAR LTD.
Hardmetal Industrial Products
Nahariya P.O.B. 34 Israel
Industrial Zone North
telephone: 04-924242
telex: 46296

ISCAR LTD.
Hardmetal Industrial Products
Nahariya P.O.B. 34 Israel
Industrial Zone North
telephone: 04-924242
telex: 46296

USA
Iscar Metals Inc.
General Office, 410 Raritan Center
Edison, N.J. 08817, POB 554
Phone (201) 225 2800, Telex 844543

USA
Iscar Metals Inc.
Branch Office,
3966 Lansdale Rd.University Heights
Ohio 44118, Phone (216) 321 4045

WEST GERMANY
Iscar Hartmetall GmbH
7500 Karlsruhe 1, Kriegsstr. 45
Postfach 3463, Phone 07 21/2 85 15
Telex 782623 isca d

1

USA
ISCAR METALS Inc.
General Office, 410 Raritan Center
Edison, N.J. 08817, POB 554
Phone (201) 225 2800, Telex 844543

USA
ISCAR METALS Inc.
Branch Office, Forest Hill Manor
2455 Lee Blvd., Cleveland Heights
Ohio 44118, Phone (216) 321 4045

WEST GERMANY
ISCAR HARTMETALL GmbH
7500 Karlsruhe 1, Kriegsstr. 45
Postfach 3463, Phone 07 21/2 85 15
Telex 782623 isca d

2

WITH COMPLIMENTS

ISCAR LTD.
Hardmetal Industrial Products
Nahariya P.O.B. 34 Israel
Industrial Zone North
telephone: 04-924242
telex: 46296

3

ISCAR LTD.
Hardmetal Industrial Products
Nahariya P.O.B. 34 Israel
Industrial Zone North
telephone: 04-924242 telex: 46296

4

5

10th maccabiah
israel 12-21.7.77 באב ו תמוז כו תשל"ז ישראל
המכביה ה

10th Maccabiah Games
Athletic competition
Dan Reisinger Designs
Designer: Dan Reisinger
Tel Aviv, Israel

The 10th Maccabiah games
is an international
Jewish sporting event
which takes place every
fourth year in Israel. This
symbol was applied to the
Maccabiah poster, on all
Maccabiah publica-
tions as well as medals,
certificates and advertising
items.

DAN REISINGER

Tokyo Tomin Bank
Designer: Shigeo Fukuda
Tokyo, Japan

On the basis of the basic idea of a 'bank which co-exists with the regional society', the elements of this mark were super-imposing the 'T' of Tokyo and Tomin on the arrow type symbols representing the people who gather in the banks. It can be called a work in which another form created by special forms overlapping each other has become another element of the design.

These plans were aggressively carried out by the Tokyo Tomin Bank's Business Department's Planning Group and centered on K.K. Space.

1

2

3

4

**Hokkaido Takushoku
Bank**
Designer: Shigeo Fukuda
Tokyo, Japan

The Hokkaido Takushoku
Bank desired that a star be
used the design theme. The
star is already a widely used
symbol, and the funda-
mental reason behind the
new star design was a
desire to freshly represent
this familiar symbol. This
desire was translated into
this symbol in which the
peak of the star was stretch-
ed up into a direction-
pointing arrow. This arrow
was then enclosed in a
circle so that the star is also
seen as a tree, which
symbolizes the bank's will
to grow and improve itself
in the future. This design
was conceived by Asahi
Kokoku-sha Co., Ltd.

Asahi Culture Center
Adult school
Designer: Shigeo Fukuda
Tokyo, Japan

The Asahi Culture Center,
which was established as
a culture project of the
Asahi Shimbun newspaper,
was a plan covering a very
wide curriculum on the
basis of the basic idea of
education and self-
development of full
fledged members of
society. Consequently, it
was concluded that it
would be impossible to
symbolize the center in a
concrete form, and the
designing was carried out
with a human being going
forward in good health.

RISO

**Riso Kagaku
Corporation**
Mimeograph company
Designer: Shigeo Fukuda
Tokyo, Japan

Riso Kagaku Corporation
is a company which is
continuing to renovate,
research and develop the
technology of the mimeo-
graph machine as a new
simple communication
tool.

1

2

Tenjin Core

Shopping department
Designer: Shigeo Fukuda
Tokyo, Japan

This symbol mark was designed on the basis of the principle of a polysemous form within an optical illusion form. In the circle, there is 'T', the initial of Tenjin. The profiles of two people facing each other form the 'T', and the two people facing each other symbolize a place of communication and meeting. Tenjin Core is a shopping building containing speciality shops, and the symbol mark was designed to introduce tender youthfulness into a clear-cut form because of the fashionable nature of the interior of the building. Many applications were designed by Nishitetsu Agency in Fukuoka.

1

2

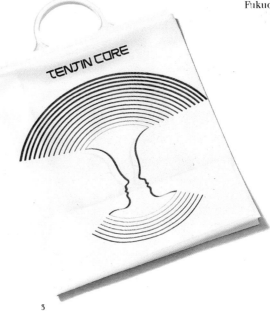

3

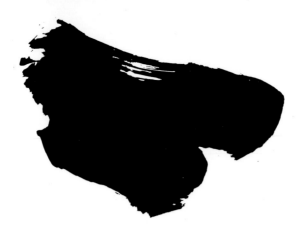

Igarashi Design
Design office
Takenobu Igarashi Design
Designer: Takenobu
Igarashi
Tokyo, Japan

The regulated repetition of
a meaningless form is
designed to function as a
mark.

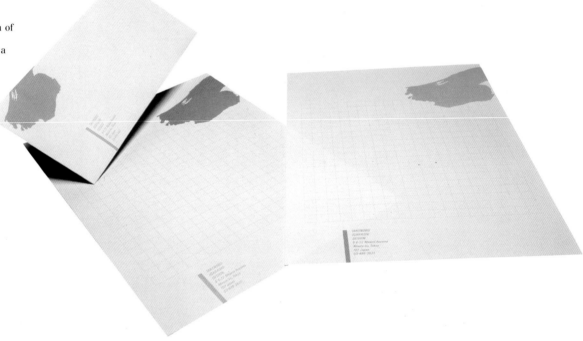

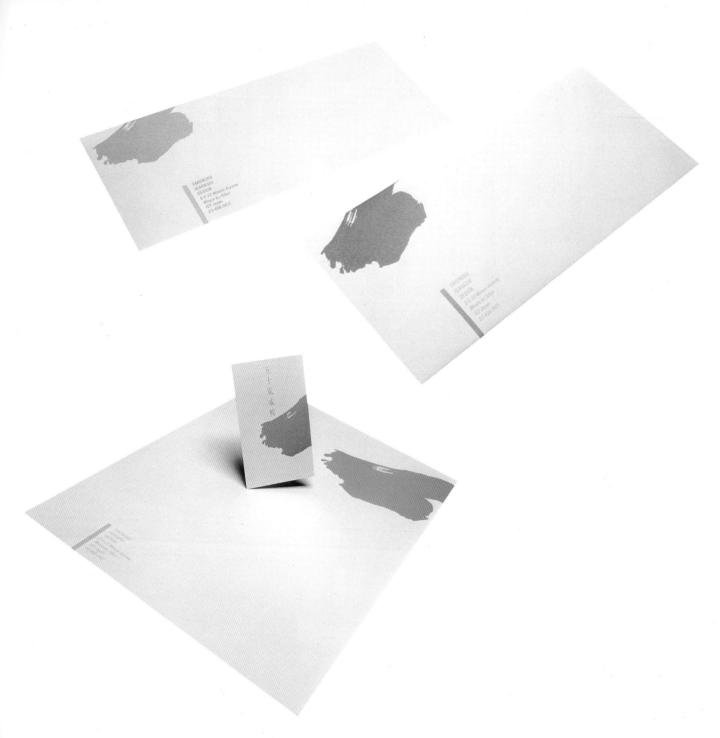

PARCO

Parco
Shopping center
Takenobu Igarashi Design
Designer: Takenobu
Igarashi
Tokyo, Japan

The logotype for a
shopping center handling
mainly interior and
sporting goods.

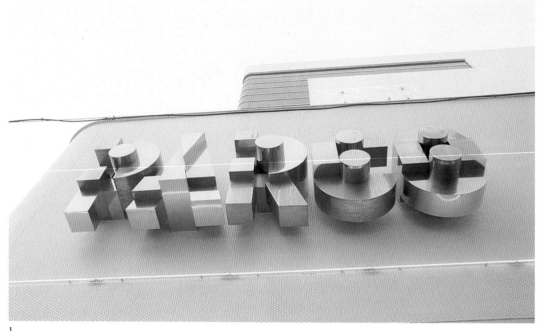

1

5

6

170

PART3

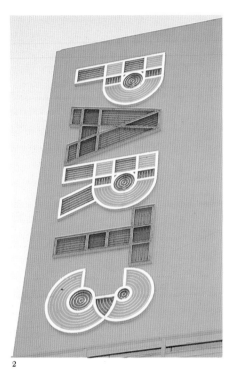

2

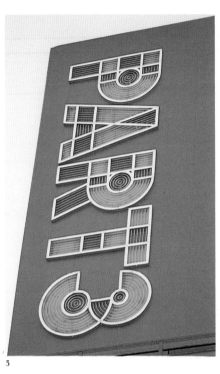

3

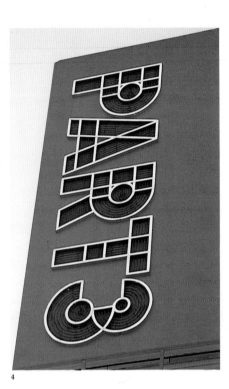

4

7

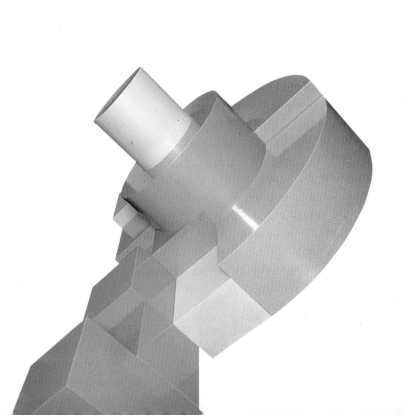

1

Summit
Super market
Takenobu Igarashi Design
Designer: Takenobu
Igarashi
Tokyo, Japan

The mark is based on the
theme of young leaves and
a tree. A 160-page manual
is available to control
design work.

2

3

4

5

KIT
Kanazawa Institute of
Technology
Takenobu Igarashi Design
Designer: Takenobu
Igarashi
Tokyo, Japan

The symbol is a combina-
tion of an aronym KIT
(Kanazawa Institute of
Technology) and a bird
designated by Ishikawa
Prefecture as the
prefectural bird. A manual
is available to control
design systems for printed
materials and signage.

Typographics T
Symbol for Japan
Typography Association's
magazine
Takenobu Igarashi Design
Designer: Takenobu
Igarashi
Tokyo, Japan

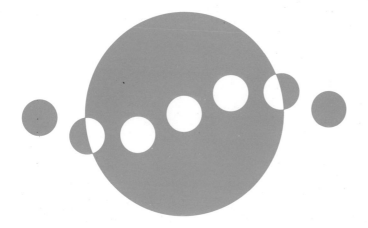

Calpis
Food industry.
Takenobu Igarashi Design
Designer: Takenobu
Igarashi
Tokyo, Japan

The composition of eight
circles symbolizes the
corporate philosophy and
ideals.

Nippon Recruit Center
Designer: Yusaku Kamekura
Tokyo, Japan

Nippon Recruit Center is a
major employment informa-
tion service agency. When
inaugurated, it was a small
company with an average
employee age of only 24.
This youthfulness was
expressed through the use
of a seagull in their symbol.
The identity program also
included the design of
signage for their new
building in Ginza, Tokyo.

1

2

3

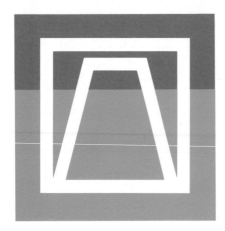

Fuji Bank
Designer: Yusaku Kamekura
Tokyo, Japan

The bank's mark is based
on the figure of Mt. Fuji.
The one-third blue and two-
thirds green color
combination gives an
impression of freshness and
youthfulness. This color
scheme applies not only to
signboards and the interior
of the bank, but also to
printed materials and
stationery. The program was
planned and produced by
Mr. Tatsu Matsumoto's
Communicatons Engineers
Co. and GK Industrial
Design Associates.

1

2

Spring

Summer

Autumn

Winter

Appi Kougen
Resort facilities
Designer: Yusaku
Kamekura
Tokyo, Japan

This symbol was designed
for a ski resort at Appi
Kougen in Iwate, Japan.
The complex will include
a hotel, pension village, as
well as ski facilities. Appi
Kougen is beautiful during
all four seasons of the
year, and this was the
basis for their identity
program. The winter and
summer symbols were
used for their winter and
summer posters, and the
different seasons were
emphasized systematically,
yet playfully.

ICSID '73
International Council of
Societies of Industrial
Designers
Designer: Yusaku Kamekura
Tokyo, Japan

ICSID was founded in
London in 1957 with the
participation of 10 countries
and 12 societies. This international design conference
took place in Kyoto in 1973.
Designed in 1971, the idea
for the conference's symbol
called for the letters 'ICSID'
to be initially surrounded by
small circle whose number
and size gradually grew
with the approach of the
conference. The growth was
climaxed by the production
of posters showing a circle
revolving around the
symbol's circles.

1

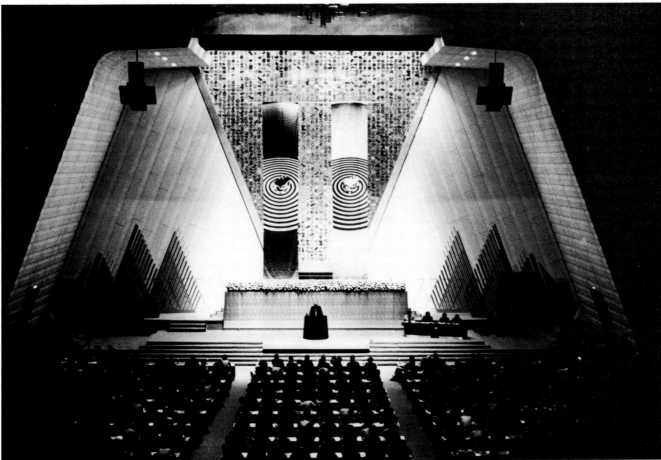

2

3

4

**International Ocean
Exposition, Okinawa
1975**
Ocean exposition
Nippon Design Center
Designer: Kazumasa Nagai
Tokyo, Japan

International Ocean
Exposition, Okinawa 1975
A simplification of
woodblock print artist
Hokusai's waves were
used as the bais for this
symbol. Three waves lined
up next to each other
gives the feeling of a vast
ocean, and the different
shades of blue express the
freshness of the sky and
sea.

**Sapporo Winter
Olympics 1972**
Winter olympics
Nippon Design Center
Designer: Kazumasa Nagai
Tokyo, Japan

The first winter Olympics
held in Japan was during
1972. The mark for the
Olympics was derived
from the red sun of the
Japanese flag combined
with snow crystals and
Olympic symbol. The
crystals were arranged to
form a Japanese crest. The
three units can be stacked
vertically or lined up
horizontally.

1

2

3

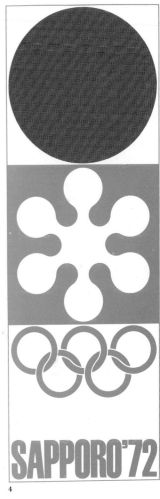

4

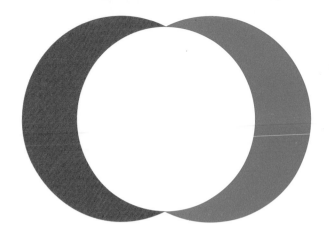

Sakura Color
Konishiroku Photo Inc., Co.
Nippon Design Center
Designer: Kazumasa Nagai
Tokyo, Japan

Konishiroku Photo Inc., Co.
is a maker of film and
cameras. The logo was
based on eye and lenses.
The circle outlined within
the red and blue arcs,
stressed the importance of
looking.

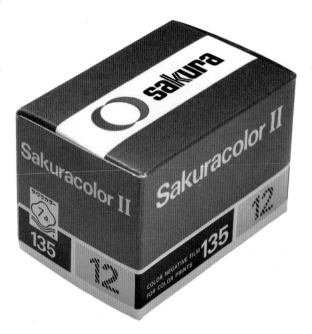

Nichii
Shopping department
Nippon Design Center
Designer: Kazumasa Nagai
Tokyo, Japan

The Nichii Co., Ltd. is a
shopping department
chain with many stores. A
dove with a four-leaf
clover is the motif.

Suruga Bank
Nippon Design Center
Designer: Kazumasa Nagai
Tokyo, Japan

Suruga Bank is located in
the city of Numazu, facing
Mt. Fuji with Suruga Bay
to one side. The symbol
combines Mt. Fuji with the
waves of Suruga Bay. The
upward movement of the
waves indicates the future
development of the bank.

Keicho
Computer data processing
company
Nippon Design Center
Designer: Kazumasa Nagai
Tokyo, Japan

Keicho is involved in computer data processing and
software. The symbol
came from the idea of
accuracy in data
processing, and it shows
the input of a white line,
the information processed
and its precise upward
movement.

Kirin Beer
Brewing company
Paos Inc.
Designers: Paos Inc.
Tokyo, Japan

The brand mark of Kirin
Beer is based on the
legendary good luck
animal of the Orient, the
'kirin' (fiery horse). Ever
since it was originally
designed in 1889, it has
established an unshake-
able position in the life
culture of the Japanese
people because of its
individual character. It is a
mark appropriate for a
company which has a
share of more than 60
percent of the market in
Japan and which is the
third largest beer brewer
in the world.

It was decided to forma-
tively refine the mark by
making this big estab-
lished value conform more
with the advancing times.
Under the design policy of
'newness taking into
consideration oldness,' a
thorough revision was
carried out while giving
adequate consideration
marketability and
development possibilities.
Furthermore, three basic
development patterns were
designed so that this
worthy mark can be used
systematically used on all
packages and related
itmes.

The aim for the whole
process was the
development of the BI
strategy of trying to
further strengthen the
appeal of the Kirin Beer
brand amid the fiercely
diversifying beer market
with the 'image age' in the
background.

1

2

4

3

Koiwai Dairy Products Co., Ltd.
Daily products company
Paos Inc.
Designers: Paos Inc.
Tokyo, Japan

The Koiwai Dairy Products Co., Ltd. introduced a new brand identity and completely changed the package designs for cheese and butter in the end of 1976. Actualizing the image assets of Koiwai of over 80 years of tradition, natural, hand-made, high-quality products and trustworthiness, a communication concept was drafted while giving consideration to distinction from a competing society, drawing-board effects and mass effects in stores. The package with classical modern, high-quality image recorded a great success on the market.

Next, at the time many new products were placed on the market in 1982, a comprehensive review was carried out on the package designs of new products and products currently on the market. As a result, while continuing the image of current packages and adding the high-quality and traditional feeling, the basic policy of 'establishment of the Koiwai special brand' was decided. What resulted was a design with a triangle in the upper left-hand corner and with the year 1893, the year the farm was established, clearly noted.

1

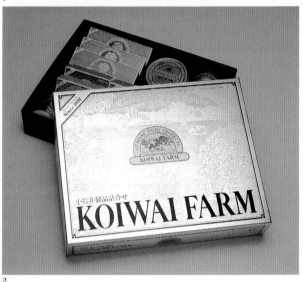

2

3

KENWOOD

Torio-Kenwood Corp.
Company of audio
equipment
Paos Inc.
Designers: Paos Inc.
Tokyo, Japan

The Trio-Kenwood Corp.,
which was established in
1946, is internationally
known as a maker of
audio equipment, amateur
wireless equipment and
measuring instruments.
The new CI system
introduced in 1982 was
carried out as a strategy
for changing the image of
the company with the
change in management as
the opportunity. The
company had been using
the two corporate brands
of 'Trio' and 'Kenwood',
but the basic policy was
decided of using one
brand, "Kenwood,"
throughout the world.

The design of the logo-
type, which is the core of
the new system, has a
triangle—continuation of
the Trio concept—as the
visual point of the letter
'W'. It symbolizes the three
key words—high quality,
advanced nature and
sharpness—which are the
concepts for creating a
new image for the
company. Furthermore, a
deformed stripe design
has been added as a sub-
element, which is a
condensation of the image
of the spreading out of
sound, to the triangle,
making it possible to carry
out wide-scope develop-
ment of the design.

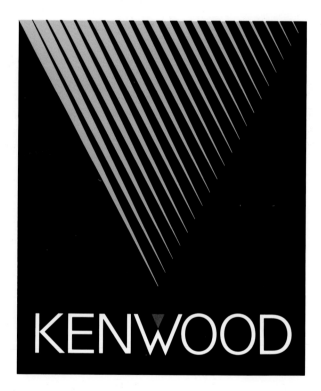

1

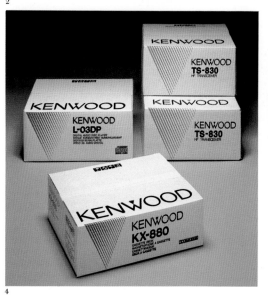

2

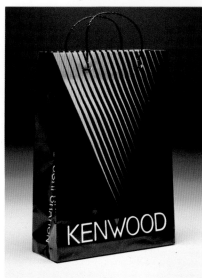

3

4

5

Hanae Mori
Symbol of costume
designer
Ikko Tanaka Design Studio
Designer: Ikko Tanaka
Tokyo, Japan

The Hanae Mori Building
designed by Kenzo Tange
was completed on the
Omotesando Street, where
land prices are very high
in Tokyo, in 1978. Ikko
Tanaka participated in the
sign plan for the building,
and this work is the
opening symbol which is
in the form of a sharply
modern butterfly, which is
the motif of Hanae Mori.
This butterfly is used
inside the elevators,
entrance to the parking
space, banner and
shopping bags. A variation
of the mark was used in
the colorful poster for the
opening.

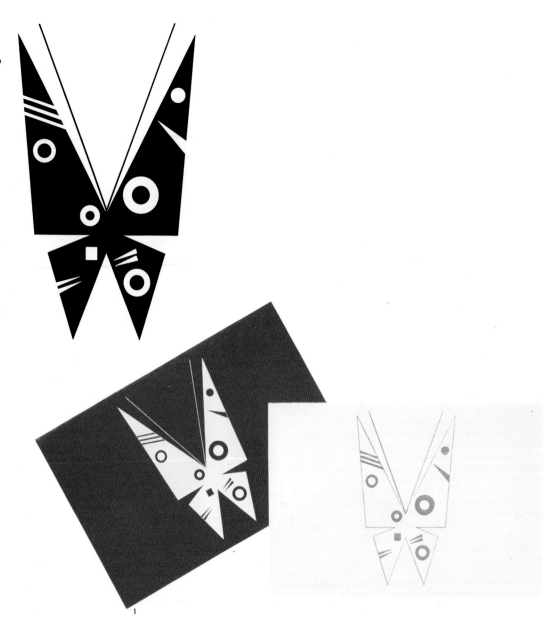

1

2

190

HANAE
MORI

**Expo '85 Tsukuba
Exposition**
Science exposition
Ikko Tanaka Design Studio
Designer: Ikko Tanaka
Tokyo, Japan

In designing the mark,
Tanaka considered the
future ideal images of
space, earth, man, science
and art. The tip of the
triangle symbolizes the
peak of Mt. Tsukuba; it
also symbolizes Tsukuba
about to welcome the
dawn of 21st century
science and technology.
The three sides of the
triangle symbolize the
themes of the exposition
of mankind, housing and
environment, while the
two circles parallel to each
other in the center
indicate the harmony
between man and science.

Issey Miyake
Symbol of costume
designer
Ikko Tanaka Design Studio
Designer: Ikko Tanaka
Tokyo, Japan

This is a logo mark
designed from Issey
Miyake's initials 'IM' and
used for all of Miyake's
licensed products. Since it
was to cover everything
from men's clothing to
everyday necessities, it
became a somewhat hard
form for fashion, but
among the various brands
that are on the market, it
became a distinctive mark
which people will not
become tired of. The
packaging and other
applications using this
symbol were designed by
'Studio Breakfast'.

Heart Art
Interior fablic and tools
shop
Ikko Tanaka Design Studio
Designer: Ikko Tanaka
Tokyo, Japan

Heart Art opened in a
corner of Aoyama-Dori in
1974. The company
operating this Heart Art is
Fujie Textile. The name of
Heart Art was adopted in
line with the merchan-
dising principle of
introducing functionality
an beautiful, human
warmth into interior
textiles, including
tablewares, and various
other daily necessities.

In the mark itself, the
heart pattern is combined
with the 'A' in 'ART' so that
it can read as Heart Art.
An attempt was made to
add the fancy feeling so
popular with the young
people.

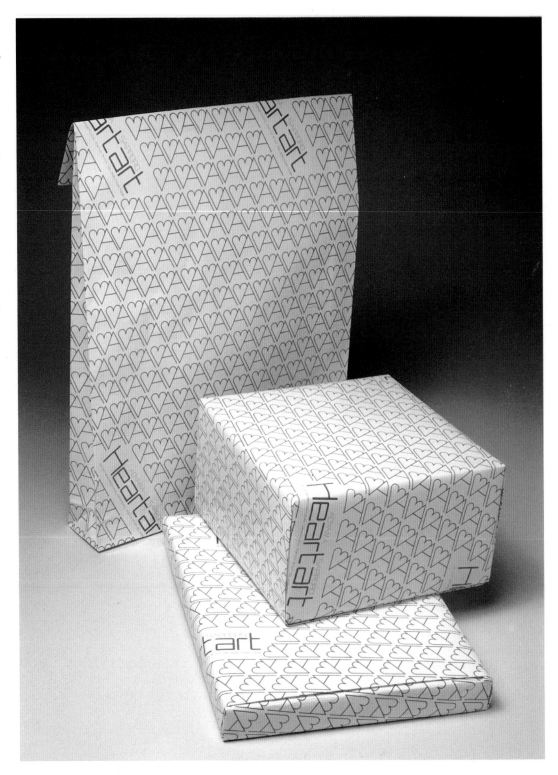

キャッシュポイント

Seibu Credit
Consumer credit company
Ikko Tanaka Design Studio
Designer: Ikko Tanaka
Tokyo, Japan

This mark is for the cash service which is one of the business lines of the company. It tries to show an image different from that of the ordinary bank, a place where the people can more easily borrow money. At the same time, it tries to express a brightness which eliminates the dark image associated with consumer credit firms in Japan. It tries to show that the money goes into individual hands, while the concentric circles in the center of the hand symbolizes the expanding dreams of individuals.

1

キャッシュポイント

2

Korea

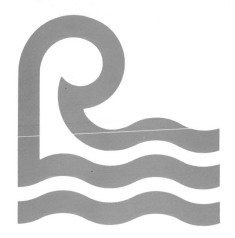

Riverside Hotel
Young Jae Cho Design
Studio
Designer: Young Jae Cho
Seoul, Korea

Cheil
Synthetic textiles
Young Jae Cho Design
Studio
Designers: Young Jae Cho,
Seung Choon Yang
Seoul, Korea

Daelim Industries
Young Jae Cho Design
Studio
Designer: Young Jae Cho
Seoul, Korea

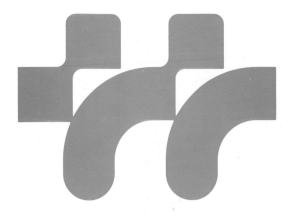

196

Dong-A
Pharmaceutical company
Young Jae Cho Design
Studio
Designers: Young Jae Cho,
Dong Jo Koo
Seoul, Korea

Korea Exchange Bank
Young Jae Cho Design
Studio
Designer: Young Jae Cho
Seoul, Korea

**The Citizens National
Bank**
Young Jae Cho Design
Studio
Designer: Young Jae Cho
Seoul, Korea

Shinsegae
Department store
Young Jae Cho Design
Studio
Designer: Young Jae Cho
Seoul, Korea

Samlip
Food manufacturer
Young Jae Cho Design
Studio
Designers: Young Jae Cho,
Dong Jo Koo
Seoul, Korea

**Korea Merchant
Banking Corporation**
Financial banking
business
Young Jae Cho Design
Studio
Designer: Young Jae Cho
Seoul, Korea

Koza Building
Social housing project
San Grafik
Designer: Mengü Ertel
Istanbul, Turkey

**Turkish Radio and
Television Writers and
Press Association**
San Grafik
Designer: Mengü Ertel
Istanbul, Turkey

Muhsin Ertuğrul
San Grafik
Designer: Mengü Ertel
Istanbul, Turkey

This design was developed to commemorate Muhsin Ertuğrul, the founder of modern Turkish theater, and his 60th year of active theater work.

Chapter IV

Australia

Australia
New Zealand

Australia

Queensland
National Parks and
Wildlife Service
Bryce Design Consultants
Designers: Michael Bryce,
Bryce Design Consultants
Queensland, Australia

The Queensland National
Parks and Wildlife Service
is responsible for the
management and conser-
vation of all National
Parks in the State of
Queensland. Bryce Design
Consultants have been
involved in the design of
their corporate identity
and signage programs
since the inception of the
service in 1975.

The adopted symbol
represents two elements:
the circle and bar which is
the international mark
of ecology; and the
Herbert River Ringtalk
Possum, an endangered
species.

1

National Parks
of Southern Coastal
Queensland

1

National Parks
of Central Coastal
Queensland

2

National Parks
of Northern Coastal
Queensland

3

2   3   4

Brisbane!

Brisbane!

Brisbane Visitors and Convention Bureau
Brisbane City Hall
GPO Box 1434
Brisbane
Australia 4001
Brisbane! Telephone 07 221 8411

Brisbane Visitors and Convention Bureau
Brisbane City Hall
GPO Box 1434
Brisbane
Australia 4001
Brisbane! Telephone 07 221 8411
Brisbane Visitors and Convention Bureau Limited
Incorporated in Queensland

Brisbane
Visitors and convention
bureau
Bryce Design Consultants
Designers: James Grose,
Bryce Design Consultants
Queensland, Australia

The Brisbane Visitors and
Convention Bureau is an
organization concerned
with the promotion of
Brisbane city in the
convention marketplace.
In 1982 a new corporate
identity was designed to
provide a stronger visual
impact in an extremely
competitive industry.

The koala was chosen to
represent the city of
Brisbane. Symbol applica-
tions have included
stationery, brochures,
posters, annual reports,
decals, convention kits
and display graphics.

Arts Victoria '75
Festival for the Arts
Ken Cato Design Company
Designer: Ken Cato
Melbourne, Australia

A state wide festival of the visual arts

Arts Victoria 75

exhibitions and activities in

Melbourne
Ararat
Ballarat
Benalla
Bendigo
Castlemaine
Geelong
Hamilton
Horsham

Langwarrin
Mildura
Mornington
Morwell
Sale
Shepparton
Swan Hill
Warrnambool

24 March
15 November
1975

1

2

Victorian Arts Centre Trust

Victorian Arts Centre Trust
Ken Cato Design Company
Designer: Ken Cato
Melbourne, Australia

1

THE SPIRE

The spire could well become Melbourne's long sought landmark. It is an open lattice space frame made of steel and aluminium, and will rise 115 metres above the St Kilda Road level. The open design was chosen to meet aerodynamic and aesthetic criteria.

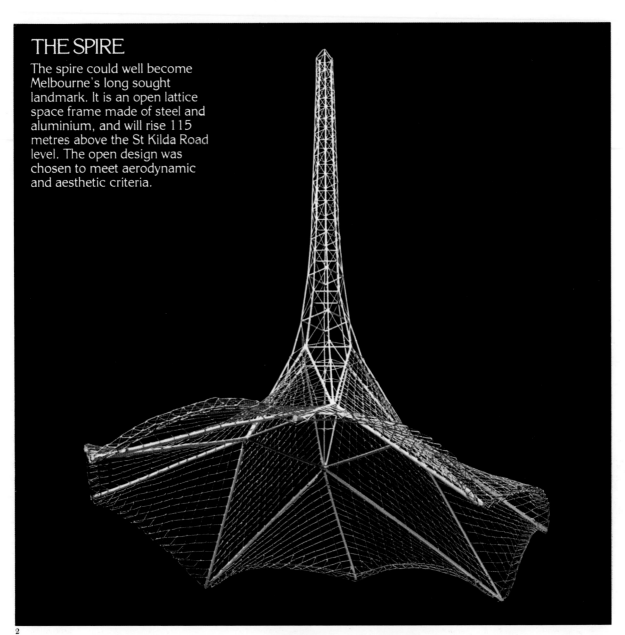

2

MELBOURNE CONCERT HALL

OPENING NOVEMBER 1982

4

5

3

Consolidated Electronic Industries

Consolidated Electronics Industries
Ken Cato Design Company
Designer: Ken Cato
Melbourne, Australia

breaking the
sound barriers

Consolidated
Electronic
Industries

Mono
Cartridge
Systems

breaking the
sound barriers

Consolidated   Reel to Reel
Electronic   Tape Systems
Industries

2

breaking the
sound barriers

Consolidated   Stereo
Electronic   Cartridge
Industries   Systems

3

4

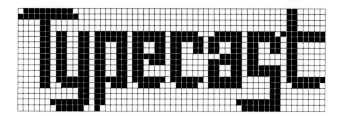

Typecast
Computer typesetter
Emery Vincent Associates
Designers: Garry Emery,
Ken Stanley, Peter Hendrie
Victoria, Australia

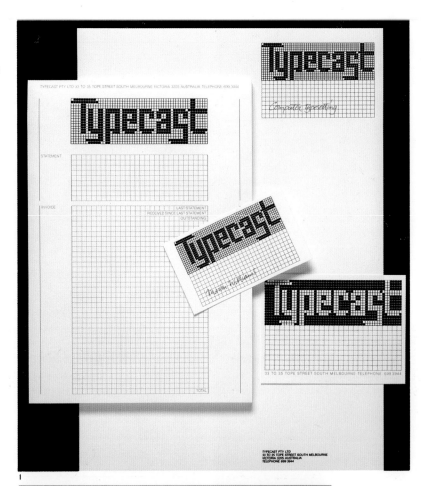

1

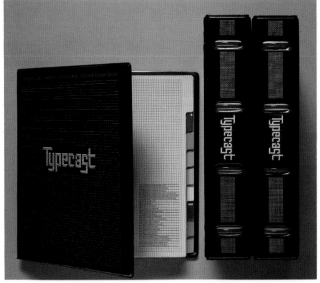

2

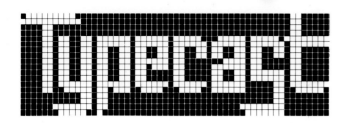

3

4

5

Cambec
Printing company
Flett Hendersen & Arnold
Designers: Flett Hendersen
& Arnold
Victoria, Australia

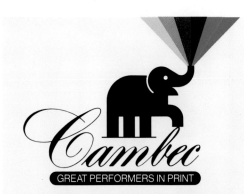

429 6144

1

2

Cambec Press Pty Ltd

19 Koornang Road
Scoresby 3179
Victoria Australia
Telephone 03 7635422
Telex AA 34258

3

Cambec Press Pty Ltd

Michael Morrison

Sales Division

Alma' 663 Victoria Street
Abbotsford 3067
Victoria Australia
Telephone 03 429 6144

4

Victoria's 150th Anniversary Celebrations 1984-5

Chairman: Sir John Holland
Executive Director: John L. Birrell

18th Floor   Collins Place   Melbourne Victoria 3000
Collins Tower   35 Collins Street   Telephone (03) 654 4144

Growing Together

Growing Together

Victoria's 150th Anniversary Celebrations 1984-5

Objectives

1. To create an awareness amongst all Victorians of their history in its broadest sense and their heritage.
2. To celebrate the richness of diversity in people, their traditions, their culture, their recreation and the precious freedoms which they enjoy.
3. To make people aware of the growth and potential of Victoria and to provide the motivation which will inspire our people with a common purpose to serve the community and plan a better future.
4. To create an awareness amongst Victorians of the opportunities available to them to enjoy one of the highest living standards in the world and at the same time to make significant contributions to those who are less fortunate.
5. To provide worthwhile and significant reminders of 150 years of achievement and growth.

18th Floor Collins Tower Collins Place
35 Collins Street Melbourne Victoria 3000
Telephone (03) 654 4144

Growing Together

Growing Together
Victoria's 150th
Anniversary Celebrations
Flett Hendersen & Arnold
Designers: Flett
Hendersen & Arnold
Victoria, Australia

The Australian State of
Victoria celebrates 150
years of European
settlement in 1984–85. To
publicize the event, a
symbol was created with
the theme 'Growing
Together'. The symbol
incorporates tree and leaf
shapes and a human
figure.

1

2

Victoria's 150th Anniversary Celebrations 1984-5

Chairman: Sir John Holland
Executive Director: John L. Birrell

18th Floor   Collins Place   Melbourne Victoria 3000
Collins Tower   35 Collins Street   Telephone (03) 654 4144

With compliments

Growing Together

3

4

Lansdowne Park
Flower grower
Flett Hendersen & Arnold
Designers: Flett
Hendersen & Arnold
Victoria, Australia

Lansdowne Park is a company producing flowers that are supplied to florist shops. The requirements made by the client were that the logo be distinctive, incorporating the company name and adaptable for stationery and signage. The client also wanted to emphasize the fact, that the flowers were grown, and cut for distribution.

**South Pacific Games
Western Samoa 1983**

**South Pacifi[c]
1983**
Athletic comp[...]
Flett Henders[...]
Designers: Fl[...]
Hendersen & [...]
Victoria, Aust[...]

The brief req[...]
that the exist[...]
of Polynesia[...]
major contri[...]
games be in[...]
appears in th[...]
the symbol, [...]
stylized figu[...]
number '7'.

**Park Avenue
Drycleaning**
Flett Hendersen & Arnold
Designers: Flett
Hendersen & Arnold
Victoria, Australia

An incorporated white dove
symbolizes the speedy
pick-up and delivery, and
a top-hat, for quality
service. Both elements
were combined into the
letter 'P'.

Carlton Silver Company
Flett Hendersen & Arnold
Designers: Flett Hendersen
& Arnold
Victoria, Australia

The Carlton Silver Company
manufacturers and
distributes silver items of
jewelry and household
wares.

Queensberry Mint
Flett Hendersen & Arnold
Designers: Flett
Hendersen & Arnold
Victoria, Australia

The Queensberry Mint
produces cast precious
metal items such as
jewelry and small
sculptures. The client
required a mark that
symbolized the company
and its product, and could
be stamped onto the items
as a hallmark.

Fresh flowers

These flowers were
grown in the gardens
of Lansdowne
of Park.

[...]VNE
[...])
[...]am Victoria 3644 Telephone (058) 73 5230

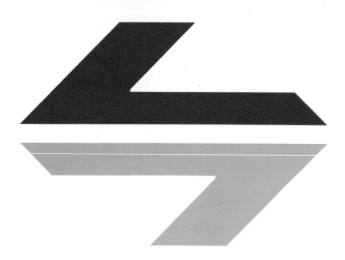

State Transport
Goodwin Design
Designers: Don Goodwin,
Sandra Buchanan
Prymont, Australia

This symbol and visual
identity was developed for
The Public Transport
Commission of New South
Wales. The organization
was set up by the New
South Wales Government
in 1972 to develop,
administer and operate the
public transport systems
within the state.

In New South Wales (NSW)
and particularly in the
metropolitan Sydney
(capital of NSW), there
exists three modes of
state-run transportation:
trains, buses and ferries.
Consequently the symbol
needed to work for all
three and become
identifiable within 'Public
Transport' overall.

1

2

3

4

217

Landmark
BUILDERS

Landmark
Solar home construction
company
Brian Sadgrove Graphic
Designer
Designer: Brian Sadgrove
Victoria, Australia

Landmark Builders Pty Ltd, 32 Rosco Drive, Templestowe, Victoria 3106 Telephone (03) 846 1422

2

1

SOLAR HOUSES

SOLAR HOUSES

79 Merton Street, Albert Park Victoria 3206

1

SOLAR HOUSES

SOLAR HOUSES

Landmark Solar Houses Pty Ltd
79 Merton Street, Albert Park, Victoria 3206,
Telephone (03) 690 5085

Landmark Solar Houses Pty Ltd
79 Merton Street, Albert Park, Victoria 3206,
Telephone (03) 690 5085

3

2

Sparrow
Children's furniture
manufacturer
Ian Hawksby Designer
Designer: Ian Hawksby
Victoria, Australia

Finnskoga
Playground equipment
manufacturer
Brian Sadgrove Graphic
Designer
Designer: Brian Sadgrove
Victoria, Australia

With Compliments

Glenwood Play Systems Pty Ltd
410 Whitehorse Road
Nunawading, Victoria, Australia 3131
Telephone (03)8734111

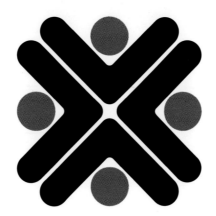

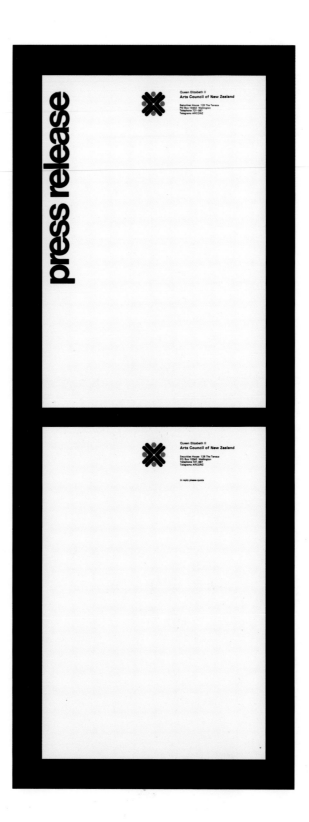

Queen Elizabeth II
Arts council of New
Zealand
Design Partners
Designer: Don Hatcher
Auckland, New Zealand

Chapter V

Western Europe

Belguim

Denmark

England

Finland

France

Italy

Netherlands

Spain

Sweden

Switzerland

West Germany

Belgium

VEV
Vlaams Ekonomisch
Verbond
Paul Ibou
Designer: Paul Ibou
Belgium

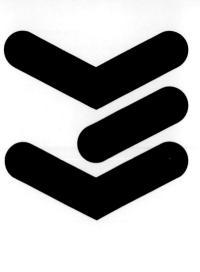

Interecho
Publisher
Paul Ibou
Designer: Paul Ibou
Belgium

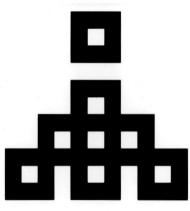

Biblo
Publisher
Paul Ibou
Designer: Paul Ibou
Belgium

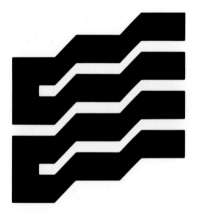

**Kon Kommer Diamonds
International**
Paul Ibou
Designer: Paul Ibou
Belgium

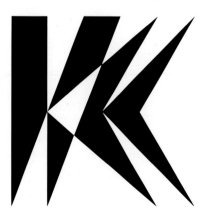

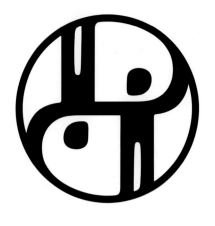

Lalique des Familles
Michel Olyff
Designer: Michel Olyff
Belgium

**Musée Royaux des
Beaux-Arts de Belgique**
Belgium Royal Museum of
Fine Arts
Michel Olyff
Designer: Michel Olyff
Belgium

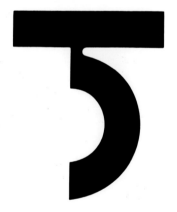

**Design Center,
Bruxelles**
Michel Olyff
Designer: Michel Olyff
Belgium

Michel Olyff, graphiste
Exhibition announcement
Michel Olyff
Designer: Michel Olyff
Belgium

Denmark

Superfos
Chemical and fertilizer
company
Papermint Design
Designer: Rolf Lagersson
Copenhagen, Denmark

1

226

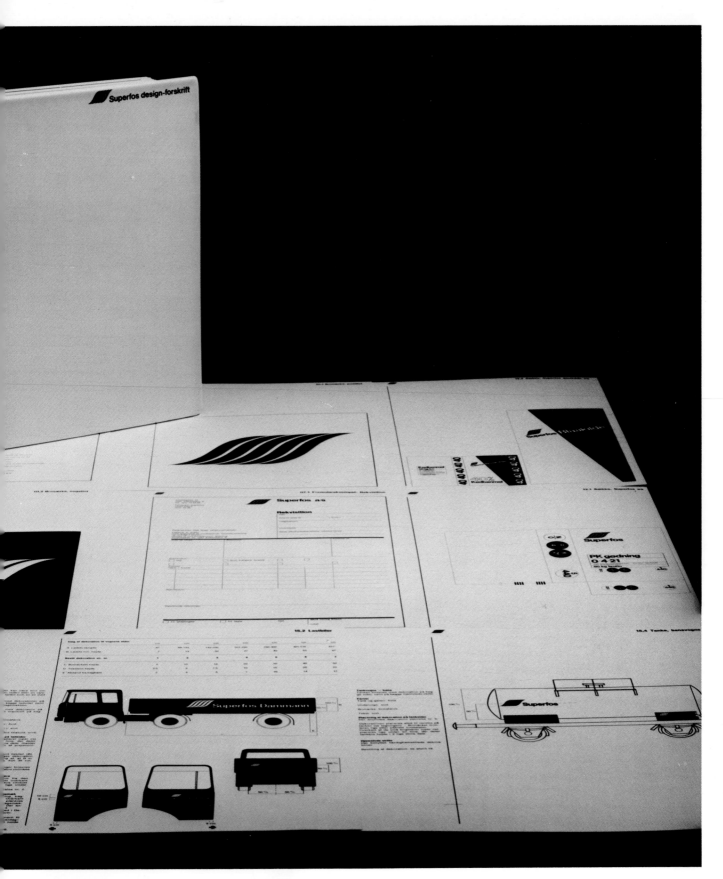

2

3

**Kay Wilhelmsen
Enterprises**
Construction company
Papermint Design
Designer: Rolf Lagersson
Copenhagen, Denmark

H. Christensen & Son
Paper company
Papermint Design
Designer: Rolf Lagersson
Copenhagen, Denmark

SC Sorenson
Hardward company
Papermint Design
Designers: C. Munch,
A. Musih
Copenhagen, Denmark

Letts of London

Letts
Diary house
WM de Majo Associates
Ltd.
Designer: WM de Majo
London, England

Charles Letts & Co Ltd,
founded in 1769, is the
world's largest publishers
of diaries. Its on-going
coordinated design
program started in 1967
when WM de Majo was
appointed Consultant
Designer. Initially the
main purpose was to re-
design and bring up to
date the company's range
of products, which
included address books,
pocket desk diaries and
calendars and other
stationery products. It was
later decided to embark
on a new corporate
identity program in which
the 'L' symbol was added
and the brand name 'Letts
of London' introduced.

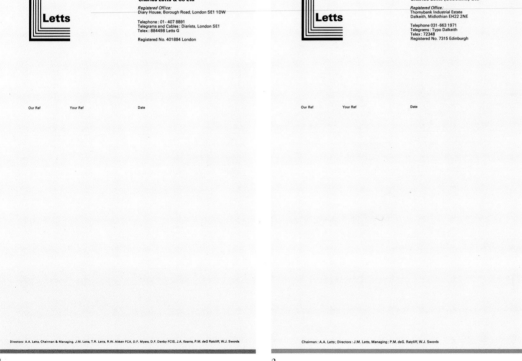

1

2

3

Amersham

1

Amersham
Radiochemical company
Henrion Ludlow &
Schmidt
Designers: Chris Ludlow,
Henrion Ludlow &
Schmidt
London, England

Amersham International
specializes in the production of radioisotopes for
medical research and
industrial applications and
had, since its establish-
ment in 1946, been known
as The Radiochemical
Centre Limited. However,
it had become known to
customers around the
world simply as
'Amersham' and had
spawned a number of
overseas subsidiaries, all
of whose names were
prefixed by 'Amersham'. It
was therefore decided that
in order to clarify the
position internationally
and create a sounder base
for marketing activities,
the name of the parent
company should be
changed to include
'Amersham'.

Henrion Ludlow &
Schmidt then produced a
concept for the inter-
relationship between the
company names and the
'Amersham' brand name
and helped to formulate
the design brief for the
visual identity part of the
project.

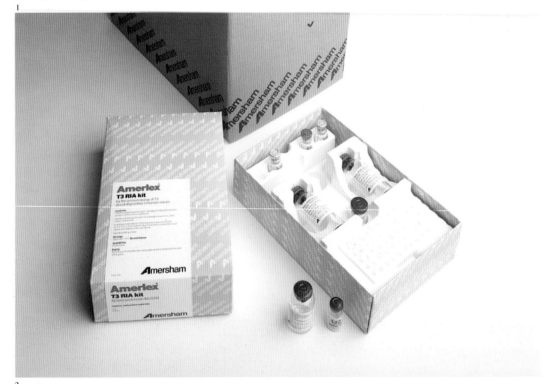

2

3

KLM
Royal Dutch Airlines
Henrion Ludlow &
Schmidt
Designers: FHK Henrion,
Henrion Ludlow &
Schmidt
London, England

The KLM housemark was
designed by Henrion
Ludlow & Schmidt to over-
come associations of old-
fashionedness and
difficulties of applications
which were inherent in
the existing mark. This
featured a realistic
representation of the
Dutch royal crown.

1

3

2

Vorwerk
Henrion Ludlow &
Schmidt
Designers: Klaus Schmidt,
Henrion Ludlow &
Schmidt
London, England

Vorwerk, based in West
Germany, was originally
known as a company
making vacuum cleaners.
Apart from the floor care
program, the Vorwerk
group diversified into
manufacturing and
marketing of pre-fab
houses, fitted kitchens,
rugs and fitted carpets,
furnishing fabrics and
thermonix equipment.
Also belonging to the
Vorwerk group are service
companies in the fields of
contract cleaning,
computer softwear service,
and information and
financial services.

1

2

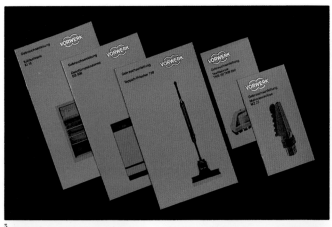

3

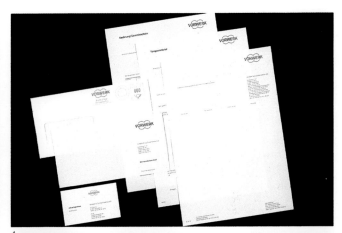

4

5

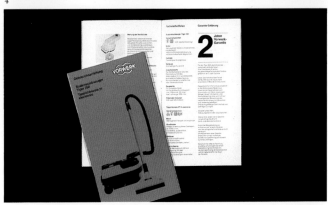

6

7

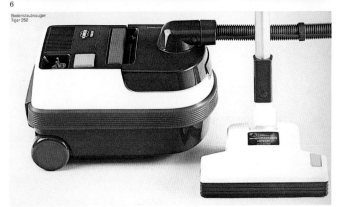

8

△
LANGERFELDT

Langerfeldt
Retail store
Henrion Ludlow &
Schmidt
Designers: Klaus Schmidt,
Henrion Ludlow &
Schmidt
London, England

Henrion Ludlow &
Schmidt was commission-
ed by Carl Langerfeldt of
West Germany to develop
a new logotype which
would correspond to the
quality consciousness of
Langerfeldt, and would be
markedly different from
the signs of competitors in
the city of Brunswick, and
would also correspond to
the accepted optical
requirements of a logo-
type. The logotype had to
do justice to Langerfeldt's
atmosphere of tradition
and reflect the customer
base, built up in the past.

The elements of the new
Langerfeldt corporate
identity combine the
traditional aspect of the
company with the
awareness of the future.
They represent quality and
efficiency. The new
corporate identity makes
the visual appearance of
Langerfeldt synonymous
with the quality of its
merchandise and overall
efficiency.

1

2

3

4

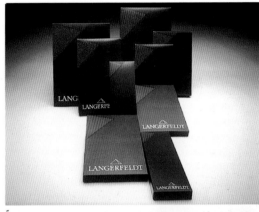

5

6

7

BDF ●●●●

BDF
Beiersdorf
Henrion Ludlow &
Schmidt
Designer: FHK Henrion
London, England

Beiersdorf AG, in
Hamburg, operates world-
wide in the manufacturing
and marketing of diverse
products. Their four
product groups (pharma-
ceuticals, surgical
dressings, cosmetics, and
industrial adhesives)
market brands such as
Nivea, Hansaplast, and
Tesa worldwide.

The aim of the corporate
identity was to make users
and the general public
alike aware of which
company was behind all of
these products. The logo is
an abbreviation of the
name Beiersdorf which
had already been used for
some time. The three
letters are clearly legible
everywhere and can be
pronounced and written in
nearly every language.
The four dots give the
company symbol a unique
and easily remembered
form. They have a modern
and simple appearance.

1

2

3

4

5

6

7

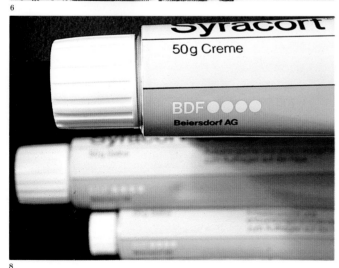

8

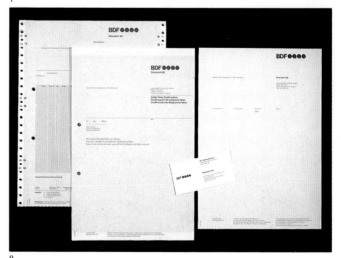

9

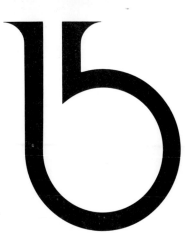

Biode
Pharmaceutical company
Lock/Pettersen Ltd.
Designer: Tor Pettersen
London, England

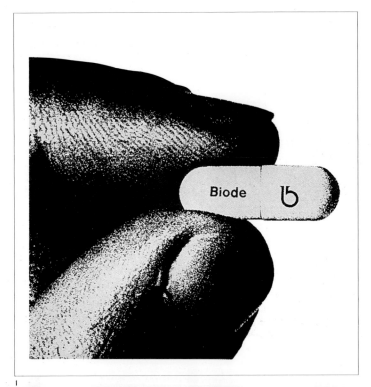

1

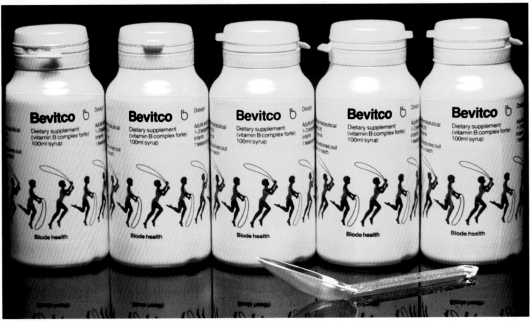

2

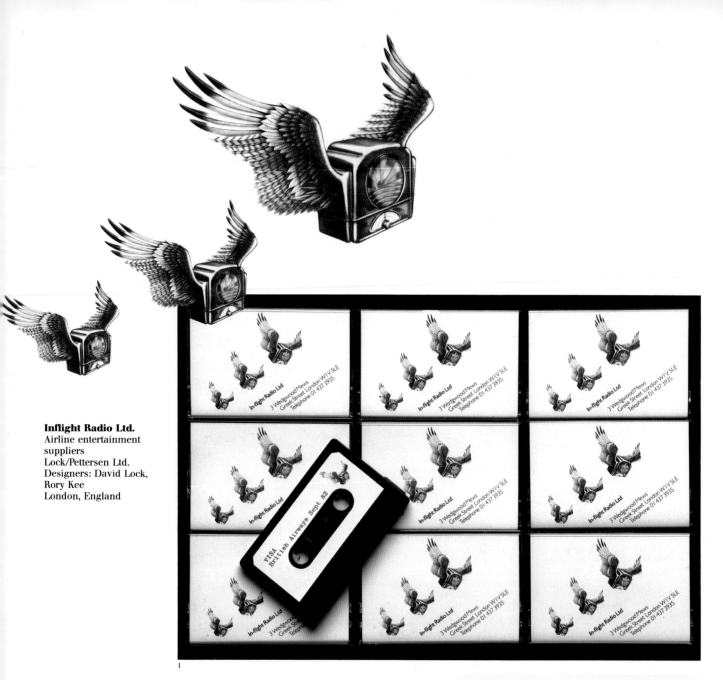

Inflight Radio Ltd.
Airline entertainment
suppliers
Lock/Pettersen Ltd.
Designers: David Lock,
Rory Kee
London, England

1

2

```
BBBBBBBBBB      AAAAAAA     RRRRRRRRRR  IIIIIIIIII  CCCCCCCCC
BBBBBBBBBBB     AAAAAAA     RRRRRRRRRR  IIIIIIIIII  CCCCCCCCCC
BBBB    BBBB    AAAAAAAAA   RRRR   RRRR   IIIII     CCCC   CCCC
BBBB    BBBB    AAAA AAAA   RRRR   RRRR   IIIII     CCCC
BBBBBBBBBB     AAAA   AAAA  RRRRRRRRRR    IIIII     CCCC
BBBBBBBBBBB    AAAA   AAAA  RRRRRRRRR     IIIII     CCCC
BBBB    BBBB  AAAAAAAAAAAA  RRRR RRRR     IIIII     CCCC
BBBB    BBBB  AAAAAAAAAAAA  RRRR   RRRR   IIIII     CCCC   CCCC
BBBBBBBBBBB  AAAA     AAAA  RRRR   RRRR  IIIIIIIIII CCCCCCCCCC
BBBBBBBBBB   AAAA     AAAA  RRRR   RRRR  IIIIIIIIII  CCCCCCCC
```

Baric
Computing services
Minale Tattersfield &
Partners
Designers: M. Minale,
B. Tattersfield,
A. Maranzano
London, England

Baric was formed in 1970
by Barcley Bank and ICL
Computers. Minale
Tattersfield & Partners was
asked to produce a
logotype that would subsequently be applied to their
corporate image.

A logotype was produced
with strong links to the
computer world. It was
based on the output of a
computer read-out sheet.
This theme became the
perfect tool for the
complete corporate image.

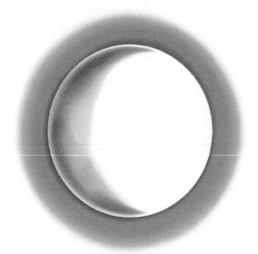

Central

Independent television company
Minale Tattersfield & Partners Ltd.
Designers: M. Minale, B. Tattersfield, A. Maranzano, D. Karavias
London, England

Central is an independent television company which began airing in Great Britain in January 1982, and replaced the old ATV Networks Ltd. The TV symbol was designed to evolve over the next ten years and lend itself to different creative interpretations, while always retaining its identity.

1

2

3

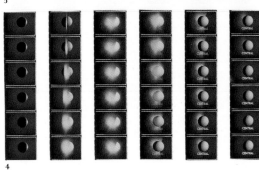

4

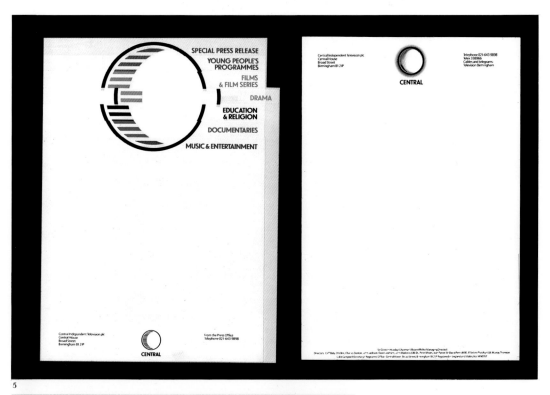

5

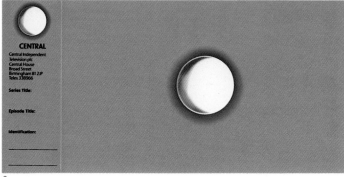

6

HEAL'S

Heal's
Department store
Minale Tattersfield &
Partners Ltd.
Designers: M. Minale,
B. Tattersfield, I. Delaney,
P. Carter
London, England

Heal's is a long established
department store with a
fine tradition of quality. In
recent years there had
been a decline in the
popularity and image of
the store. It was therefore
necessary to reassert the
quality of the past, but at
the same time bring it in
line with the present day
requirements.

A section of the original
border theme used by
Ambrose Heal (the
founder) was extracted
and introduced into the
new logotype design. The
color schemes also change
according to fashions or
trends.

1

Heal & Son limited
196 Tottenham Court Road London W1A 1BJ
Telephone 01-636 1666
Telex 267419

With compliments

2

The best of French design and culture throughout April at

HEALS

3

244

Hospital Design Partnership

Hospital Design Partnership
Architectural firm
Minale Tattersfield &
Partners Ltd.
Designers: M. Minale,
B. Tattersfield,
A. Maranzano, I. Grindle
London, England

Hospital Design Partnership is an architectural practice specializing in hospital designs worldwide. The internationally recognized red cross symbol was translated into a building, with its obvious connotations being apparent to all different countries.

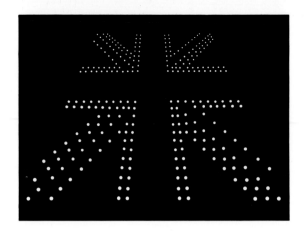

British Airports
Minale Tattersfield &
Partners Ltd.
Designers: M. Minale,
B. Tattersfield,
A. Maranzano
London, England

This symbol was designed
in 1978 for an exhibition of
British Airport Designs at
the Design Centre in
London.

1

British Airports at The Design Centre

Haymarket, London. June 19 – July 21. Open Monday – Saturday 09.30 – 17.30. Wednesday & Thursday until 21.00. Admission free

2

**Minale Tattersfield &
Partners Ltd.**
Design consultants
Minale Tattersfield &
Partners Ltd.
Designers: M. Minale,
B. Tattersfield
London, England

1

Minale, Tattersfield & Partners Limited
Burston House, Burston Road, Putney, London SW15 6AR Telephone: 01-788 8261

Minale, Tattersfield & Partners Limited
Burston House, Burston Road, Putney, London SW15 6AR Telephone: 01-788 8261
Telex: 22397 Mintat G   Design Consultants

2

MARCELLO MINALE
AN EXHIBITION OF PAINTINGS DRAWINGS AND PRINTS
Please come to the Private View on Thursday 11 June 6pm - 8pm at Graffiti 3rd floor 44 Great Marlborough St London W1 Telephone 01 437 6484 Exhibition closes Friday 26 June

3

Directors: Marcello Minale FSIAD, Brian Tattersfield ARCA FSIAD, Alex Maranzano M Des(RCA), Ian Grindle MA(RCA)
Registered Office: 143 Ebury Street, London SW1 Registered in England No 821066

4

Minale Tattersfield Designers

IDEA SPECIAL ISSUE ミナーレ・タッタースフィールド・デザイナーズ

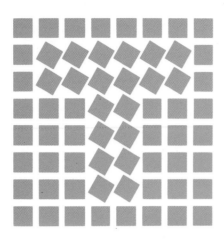

Tactics
Men's cosmetics
Pentagram
Designers: Mervyn
Kurlansky, Lora Starling
London, England

Tactics is a range of men's
cosmetics manufactured
by Shiseido, Japan. This
symbol was based on the
letter 'T', representing the
brand name Tactics, and
the design was conceived
to reflect gamesmanship.

The symbol is a square
made up of 64 spaced-out
small solid squares with
20 angled squares forming
the letter 'T'. The symbol
and the name are applied
in gold on white
containers and the black/
brown outer packs: the
product category appears
only on the container, in
gold.

**Mr. Beeton and
Mr. Tennant**
Food shop
Pentagram
Designers: John
McConnell,
Howard Brown
London, England

This symbol is for a shop
selling high-quality, home-
made foods. The cook
acting on the daily
comments that the studio
lunch was excellent
decided to leave and set
up with a friend. The
symbol was designed to
be friendly and evoke the
flavor of good home
cooking.

Fred To
Airplane company
Pentagram
Designers: John
McConnell,
John Rushworth
London, England

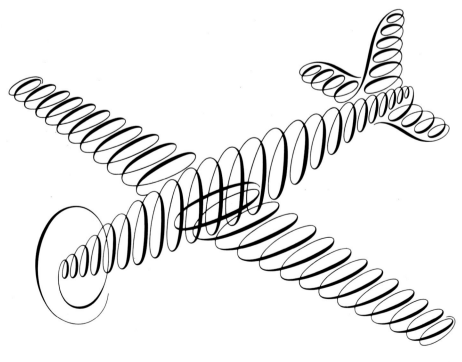

Viscom
Visual communications
Pentagram
Designers: David Hillman,
Nancy Williams, Liz James
London, England

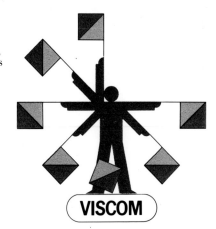

**Kent State/Pentagram
Workshop**
Graphic Design workshop
Pentagram
Designers: Mervyn
Kurlansky, Robert Maude
London, England

D&AD
Designers and Art
Directors Association
Pentagram
Designer: Colin Forbes
London, England

Cedric Lisney Associates
Architects and landscape
architects
Pentagram
Designers: David Hillman,
Nancy Williams
London, England

**Cape Boards and Panels
Limited**
Fire resistant products
Pentagram
Designers: Colin Forbes,
Jean Robert
London, England

**Zinc Development
Association**
Pentagram
Designer: Alan Fletcher
London, England

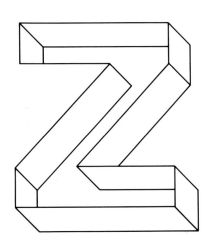

Building
Trade magazine
Pentagram
Designers: David Hillman,
Vyv Thomas,
Michael English
London, England

Building magazine is the
largest weekly trade
publication in the industry.
It was derived from the
traditional blue wall
plaques. In addition to
appearing on the cover of
the magazine, it was also
applied to a full range of
stationery, documentation
and promotional material.

Dinar
Financial magazine
Pentagram
Designers: David Hillman,
Nancy Williams
London, England

Dinar is a prestige
magazine on the interna-
tional world of finance.
Published by the
Commercial Bank of
Kuwait, it is printed in
both Arabic and English.
The logotype had to
convey both languages
and scripts.

Nobrium
Pharmaceutical product
Pentagram
Designers: Mervyn
Kurlansky,
Maddy Bennett
London, England

ADAMS

Adams
Childrenswear store
Michael Peters & Partners
Designers: Michael Peters,
Bev Whitehead,
Claire Tuthill
London, England

1

2

3

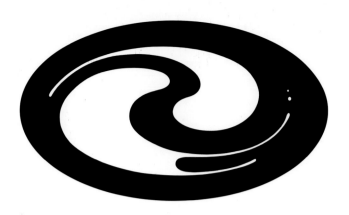

International Coffee Organization
Michael Peters & Partners
Designers: Michael Peters,
Madeline Bennett
London, England

Hawkeye
Mechanical artwork
production studio
Michael Peters & Partners
Designer: Klaus Schultheis
London, England

Marketing Solutions
Marketing and
promotional consultants
David Pocknell Company
Ltd.
Designer: David Pocknell
Essex, England

MARKETING SOLUTIONS

Marketing
Solutions
Limited
70 Salusbury Road
Queen's Park
London NW6 6NU
Telephone 01-624 6090
Directors J T Crisp (Chairman) S A Clare D H F Drakes D J Lee D M Thomas P W Watkins
Registered Office 70 Salusbury Road Queen's Park London NW6 6NU
Registered in England 1090505

MARKETING SOLUTIONS

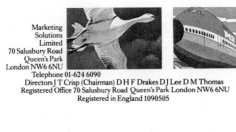

Marketing
Solutions
Limited
70 Salusbury Road
Queen's Park
London NW6 6NU
Telephone 01-624 6090
Directors J T Crisp (Chairman) D H F Drakes D J Lee D M Thomas
Registered Office 70 Salusbury Road Queen's Park London NW6 6NU
Registered in England 1090505

MARKETING SOLUTIONS

Marketing
Solutions
Limited
70 Salusbury Road
Queen's Park
London NW6 6NU
Telephone 01-624 6090

With Compliments

1

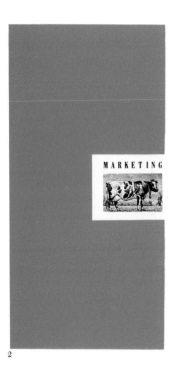

MARKETING

MARKETING SOLUTIONS

A BRIEF HISTORY

Marketing Solutions was founded in 1973 as an independent fee-based marketing and promotional consultancy, wholly owned by its working directors, which it remains to this day.

The Company opened its doors with the stated intention of providing a high professional standard of marketing and promotional advice, supported by creative excellence and highly efficient Client servicing.

Particular emphasis has always been placed on accurate problem definition and relevant commercial solutions and to fulfil this promise the Company has consistently hired in at senior level experienced and imaginative marketing people.

The concept of Marketing Solutions has proved to be extremely successful over the years since the Company's formation, and the Company's Client list bears due testimony to the regard in which the Company is held.

Interestingly, the Company has begun in recent years to attract Clients from areas other than fast-moving consumer goods, historically the Company's main area of strength, thus helping to fulfil the Directors' objective of building a balanced mix of Company Clients.

A further testimony to the Company's reputation is the long list of awards the Company has won for work conducted on its Clients' behalf.

Marketing Solutions is now a company with a turnover approaching £2 million per annum, whose balance sheet shows it to be a highly profitable, totally independent concern, owning its own substantial freehold premises.

The Company employs upwards of 40 people and is generally acknowledged to be one of the largest and best companies operating in the field of marketing and promotional consultancy in the United Kingdom.

HISTORY

MARKETING SOLUTIONS

OUR KEY PEOPLE

CHAIRMAN

Educated at Cambridge University. Seven years with the Imperial Tobacco Group cigar marketing division: managing leading brands; investigating implications of Smoking and Health legislation on cigar marketing policy; resourcing European brands. Founded Marketing Solutions in 1973.

MANAGING DIRECTOR

Educated at Cambridge University. Six years account management at Doyle Dane Bernbach Ltd. and Sharps Ltd. across a broad spectrum of product fields.

Subsequently helped set up and run for four years a small manufacturing business, producing and marketing a range of family games for the U.K. and U.S.A. markets. Joined Marketing Solutions in 1977.

DIRECTOR

Educated at Leeds University. Three years with Lever Bros Ltd. in brand management with the Soap and Household Cleaning Groups.

A further three years in account management with Allen Brady and Marsh Ltd. across a number of product areas. Joined Marketing Solutions in 1981.

DIRECTOR

Career development with Cadbury Ltd. in sales and subsequently marketing management.

Four years account management with D'Arcy MacManus and Masius on fast moving consumer goods. Joined Marketing Solutions in 1976.

DIRECTOR

Educated at Oxford University. Six years account management with Waseys Ltd. and Lintas Ltd. across a number of product fields. Moved to Courage Ltd. for three years, becoming Marketing Manager. Joined Marketing Solutions in 1977.

KEY PEOPLE

MARKETING SOLUTIONS

OUR CLIENT LIST

Allied Breweries (UK) Limited;
National Brands Development and Sales;
Bavarian Beer Importers;
Brewery Industry Sales Division;
Tetley Walker;
Ansells;
Ind Coope: East Anglia, Benskins, Friary Meux;
Taylor Walker
Bowyers Limited
British Airways
British Rail
Cadbury Limited
CBS Records
Clarks Limited
Dairy Crest Creameries
Dairy Crest Dairies
The Department of Industry;
Information Technology Division;
Posts and Telecommunications Division
The Glenlivet Distillers Limited (part of Seagram Limited)
Ladbroke Racing Limited
Mastercare (CGS Limited)
Philip Morris Limited
Schweppes Limited
Schweppes International
Shulton Limited
Wilkinson Sword

CLIENT LIST

MARKETING SOLUTIONS

ACTIVITIES UNDERTAKEN

The work undertaken on behalf of the Company's Clients is highly varied in nature, but may be categorised into two basic areas.

STRATEGIC ANALYSIS AND PLANNING

The Company is increasingly used by the majority of its Clients to help formulate marketing plans, brand (and even Company) strategies and to assist general and marketing management to plan their company's or their products' future.

SALES PROMOTION ACTIVITIES

The bedrock of the Company's business has historically been and indeed remains in the devising, running and monitoring of all those activities which may be broadly defined as "below-the-line", i.e. non-media based.

This encompasses all manner of different activities from straight trade and consumer promotions to the planning and organising of sales conferences, providing sales force material, briefing and running auxiliary sales forces, devising trade and sales force incentive schemes, and so on.

The nature of the Company's work is such that it is often the case that promotional activity needs to be supported by a limited level of media advertising. Where any of the Company's Clients are either unable or unwilling to use an advertising agency for such support activity Marketing Solutions will place it through its media brokers and devise the advertising internally.

Where sponsorship activities are relevant as part of a marketing programme, or are an integral part of commercial activities (as in the case of a sporting body) Marketing Solutions has the knowledge and expertise to advise on and run activity in this interesting and increasingly important sector of the marketing armoury.

ACTIVITIES

MARKETING SOLUTIONS

OUR TRACK RECORD

The Company submits its work to the Institute of Sales Promotion for annual judging by a panel of marketing experts, who declare awards and commendations on the twin bases of commercial effectiveness and creativity.

Marketing Solutions has won awards for its work every year since 1975, when it first submitted entries and has won the Grand Prix three times in the last six years for the best piece of activity in that year.

Listed below are the last four years' commendations and awards.

COMMENDATIONS & AWARDS, INSTITUTE OF SALES PROMOTION

1981

British Railways Board	The British Rail Journey Club Gold award for the best use of posters.
Ansells Brewery Limited	Get Into Gear with Ansells Silver award.
Department of Industry	National Teletext Month.

TRACK RECORD

2 3 4 5 6 7

Sportsmen in Business
Professional sportsmen's
company
David Pocknell Company
Ltd.
Designers: David Pocknell,
Duncan Moore
Essex, England

Sportsmen in Business is a
company aimed to exploit
their success within sports
in commercial terms. The
design program consists of
a range of stationery,
promotion brochures and
individual portfolios of
personalities including
photographs, and prsonal
data.

258

**The Commitment
Conference**
Teletex and viewdata
promotion
David Pocknell Company
Ltd.
Designers: David Pocknell,
Duncan Moore
Essex, England

The project for The
Commitment Conference
consisted of a range of
literature and conference
material produced for the
Department of Industry to
promote Teletex and
Viewdata within the tele-
vision industry.

1

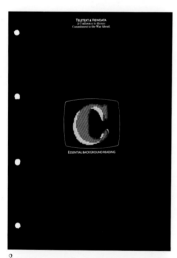

2

3

Starting with a few basic facts and
figures.

Teletext's sluggish growth: why?

Prestel's big questionmark: when
will a mass consumer market
materialize?

The critical question of cost: can it
really be brought down?

Chips, sets and adaptors: who can
look with confidence to the future?

The ominous threat of foreign
competition.

Making a real commitment to
ensuring future market growth.

4

5

6

7

bip

Bip
Family clothing store
David Pocknell Company
Ltd.
Designer: David Pocknell
Essex, England

1

Bip, 6F Sloane Street, London SW1
Telephone 01 235 3030

2

THE TEAM

BIP ● 234 EAST 60TH STREET, NEW

3

261

ARAL
Petroleum products
Wolff Olins
Designers: Michael Wolff,
David Bristow,
Gerry Barney
London, England

1

2

P&O
Land and sea transport
companies
Wolff Olins
Designers: Michael Wolff,
John Sorrell, Gerry Barney,
Kit Cooper
London, England

1

2

RENAULT

Véhicules Industriels

Renault
Wolff Olins
Designers: Michael Wolff,
Steve Howell,
Valerie Allam
London, England

1

2

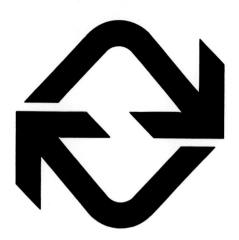

Helsinki City Transport
Studio G4
Designers: Esko Miettinen,
Anitta Kainulainen,
Noora Siivonen,
Wladmir Tomewski
Helsinki, Finland

The studio of Esko
Miettinen was commis-
sioned by the City of
Helsinki to design the
visual identity program
and trademark for their
transport system. The
Helsinki City Transport
visual identity program
consists of the color
system, the typeface, and
the conscious use of asym-
metric typography. The
color system, for historic
and technical reasons has
two types of blue and
yellow, and one orange.
The typeface chosen is
Helvetica.

The visual identity pro-
gram has been applied
systematically to all
internal and external
printed matter, such as
tickets, brochures, posters,
street furniture, interior
decorations and on
vehicles.

1

2

3

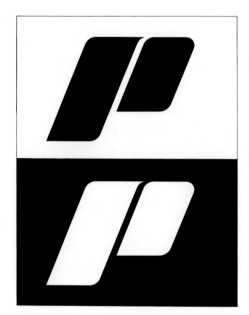

PUOLIMATKA	Liikemerkki	2
		31.8.81

1

PUOLIMATKA	Liikemerkin ja logo-tyypin suhde	7
		31.8.81

PUOLIMATKA-yhtymä Oy

2

PUOLIMATKA	PUOLIMATKA-yhtiöiden logotyypit	9
		31.8.81

PUOLIMATKA-yhtiöt

PUOLIMATKA-yhtymä Oy

PUOLIMATKA Group Ltd.

Rakennustoimisto
A. PUOLIMATKA Oy

Auttila Oy

Oulun Rakennus Oy

Seuturakennus Oy

Rakennusvalmiste Oy

Rakennusvalmiste Oy
Kiintokaluste

Puuleima Oy

Kokkosenlahden Saha Oy

3

PUOLIMATKA	Rakennusvalmiste Oy liikemerkki ja logotyyppi	23
		31.8.81

Rakennusvalmiste Oy   Rakennusvalmiste Oy   Rakennusvalmiste Oy   Rakennusvalmiste Oy

4

Puolimatka
Construction corporation
Studio G4
Designers: Esko Miettinen,
Anitta Kainulainen,
Wladimir Tomewski
Helsinki, Finland

Puolimatka is the largest
construction corporation in
Finland with activities in
Finland, the Soviet Union,
the Middle-East, Middle
Europe and the United
States.

Studio G4 was
commissioned to design
their new trademark in
1980. After year and a half
of systematic study the
trademark was designed
and approved, and the
identity program for field
use was designed.

Congrès UITP
The Congress of the
International Union of
Public Transport
Studio G4
Designers: Esko Miettinen,
Anitta Kainulainen,
Jyrki Nieminen
Helsinki, Finland

Studio G4 was commis-
sioned to design the visual
identity program for the
Congress of the Interna-
tional Union of Public
Transport held in Helsinki
in June 1979. The congress
was organized by the
Helsinki City Transport
and the project included
signage, and printed
materials such as letter-
heads, luggages labels,
lunch tickets, invitation
cards, programs, etc.

1

2

Union Internationale des Transports Publics
International Union of Public Transport
Internationaler Verband für öffentliches
Verkehrswesen

Etiquette de Bagages
Luggage Label
Anhänger für Reisegepäck

3

Déjeuner
Lunch
Mittagessen

Restaurant Finlandia

Mercredi   13 juin   1979 à   13.00 h
Wednesday June 13, 1979 at 13.00 h
Mittwoch,   13. Juni 1979 um 13.00 Uhr

Le coupon doit être remis
au serveur.
This coupon must be given
to the waiter.
Coupon bitte dem Ober
übergeben.

4

Sightseeing

Visite de la ville de Helsinki
Tour of the City of Helsinki
Besichtigung der Stadt Helsinki

Mardi 12 juin 1979 a 15.00 h
Tuesday June 12, 1979 at 15.00 h
Dienstag, 12. Juni 1979 um 15.00 Uhr

Le coupon doit être remis
au guide.
This coupon must be given
to the guide.
Coupon bitte dem Gruppen-
leiter übergeben.

5

Technical visit 9

Fabrication d'appareils de liaison radio par la
firme Oy Televa.
Production of radiophones and communication
equipment by Oy Televa.
Herstellung von Funkgeräten bei der Firma
Oy Televa.

Jeudi   14 juin   1979 14.00 — 17.00 h
Thursday   June 14, 1979 14.00 — 17.00 h
Donnerstag, 14. Juni 1979 14.00 — 17.00 Uhr

Le coupon doit être remis
au guide.
This coupon must be given
to the guide.
Coupon bitte dem Gruppen-
leiter übergeben.

7

ServiSystems
Cleaning company
Varis Poteri Veistola Oy
Designer: Kyösti Varis
Helsinki, Finland

Kaitilan Kutomo Oy
Weaving works
Varis Poteri Veistola Oy
Designer: Kyösti Varis
Helsinki, Finland

Finnair
Airline
Varis Poteri Veistola Oy
Designer: Kyösti Varis
Helsinki, Finland

Amer-tupakku
Tobacco company
Varis Poteri Veistola Oy
Designer: Kyösti Varis
Helsinki, Finland

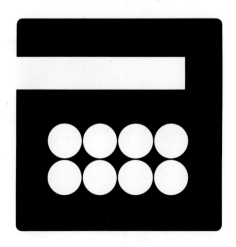

FILMITALLI

Filmitalli/Film Stable
Veistola Oy
Designer: Jukka Veistola
Helsinki, Finland

Fazer Catering
Catering service
Veistola Oy
Designer: Jukka Veistola
Helsinki, Finland

J. Muller Catering
Catering service
Veistola Oy
Designer: Jukka Veistola
Helsinki, Finland

France

Maillet Expositions
Exhibition construction
Bureau d'Etudes
Garamond
Designers: R. Kate
Garamond,
Jacques Garamond
Anet, France

les établissements
Maillet-Expositions
vous présentent
leurs vœux les meilleurs
pour la
nouvelle année

75

2

1

Ferme de Châteauneuf
Guyancourt, 78000 Versailles

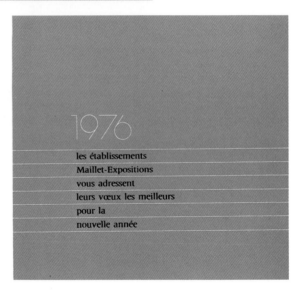

1976

les établissements
Maillet-Expositions
vous adressent
leurs vœux les meilleurs
pour la
nouvelle année

3

4

Cie Air France
Airline
Bureau d'Etudes
Garamond
Designers: R. Kate
Garamond,
Jacques Garamond
Anet, France

This new design of the
traditional label is used in
the Editions department
for use on house-organs,
annual reports, com-
mercial cards, greetings,
etc.

Merlin Gerin
Electrical power systems
Technes
Designer: Gérard Guerre
Seine, France

1

2

Locamion

Locamion
Industrial vehicles
Technes
Designer: Gérard Guerre
Seine, France

1

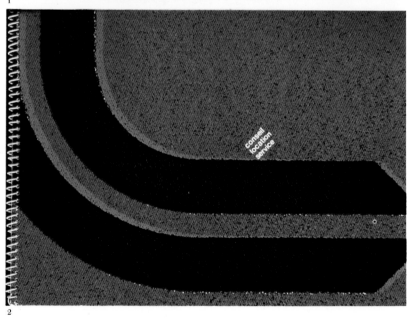

conseil
location
service

2

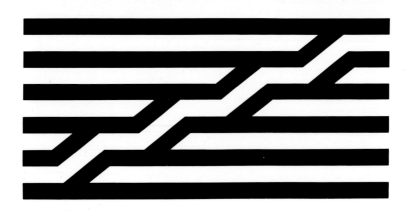

Centre Georges Pompidou
National Center of Art and Culture
Visuel Design
Designers: Jean Widmer, Ernst Heistand
Paris, France

The color code for the organization of different departments in the building are: Yellow: George Pompido National Center for Art and Culture. Blue: Industrial Design Center. Red: National Museum of Art. Green: Public Information Library. Violet: Institute for Research and Arrangement of Musical Sounds (IRCAM).

1

2

3

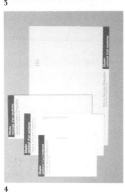

4

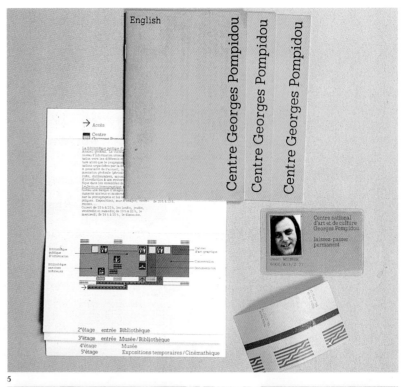

5

6

7

9

10

11

8

12

Kieler Woche 1980   21.–29. Juni

Kieler Woche 1980
Annual nautical festival
Visuel Design
Designer: Jean Widmer
Paris, France

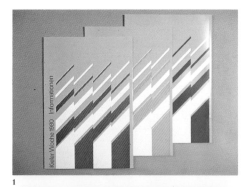

1

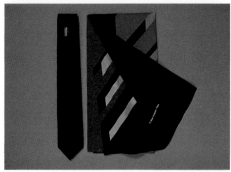

2

Kieler Woche 1980   21.–29. Juni

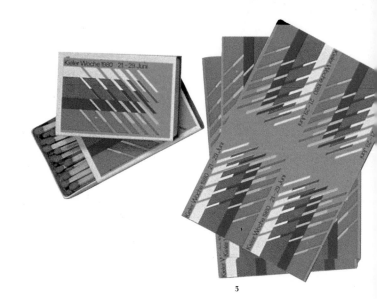

3

Einladungen

Einladung

Einladung

Eröffnung
der Kieler Woche
Sonnabend, 21. Juni

Einladung

Regattabegleitfahrt
Mittwoch, 25. Juni

Einladung

Kieler Woche-Tag
für das Konsular-Korps
Dienstag, 24. Juni

Kieler Woche 1980   21.–29. Juni

Kieler Woche 1980   21.–29. Juni

4

5

6

**Animation Touristique
des Autoroutes**
Tourist information for
freeways
Visuel Design
Designer: Jean Widmer
Paris, France

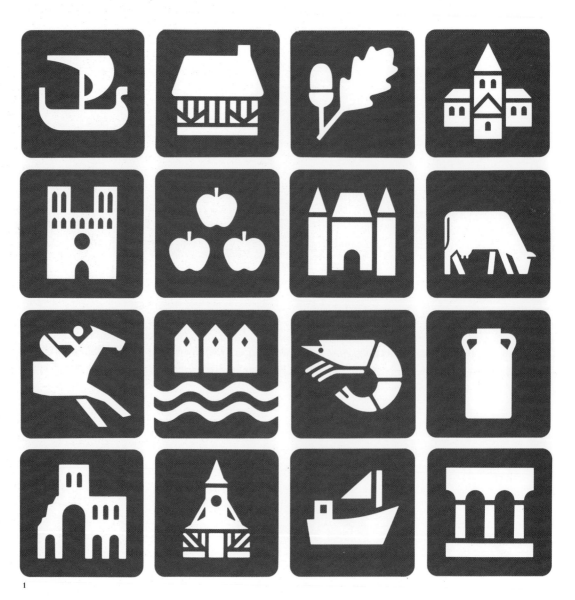

1

2

3

Varian
Electronics components
corporation
Gruppo Signo
Communicazione Totale
Designer: Giulio Cittato
Venice, Italy

1

2

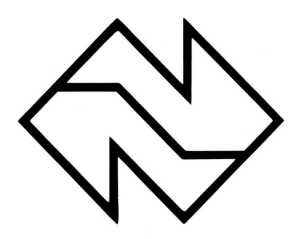

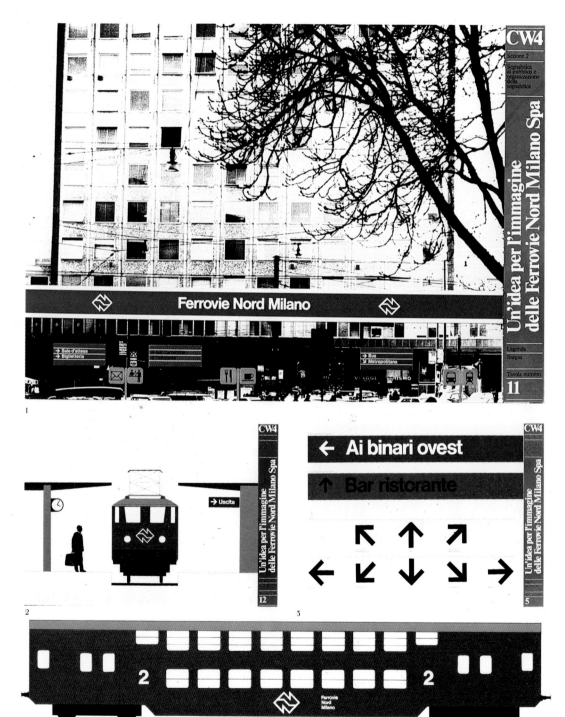

Mirano Ferrovie nord I.D.
Gruppo Signo
Designers: Giulio Cittato,
Heinz Waibl
Miran, Italy

Acnil

Acnil
Venice public
transportation system
Gruppo Signo
Communicazione Totale
Designer: Giulio Cittato
Venice, Italy

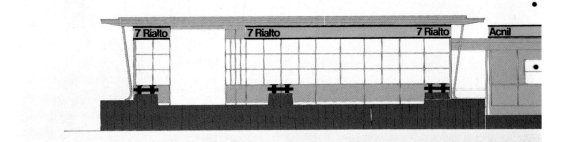

1

3

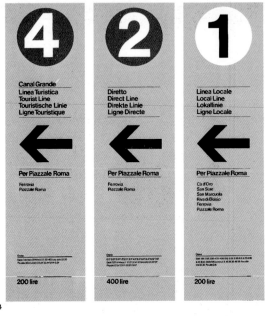

4

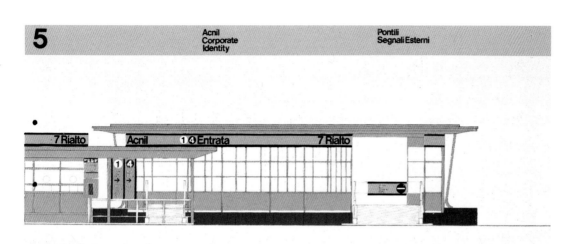

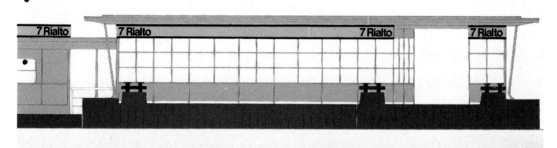

2

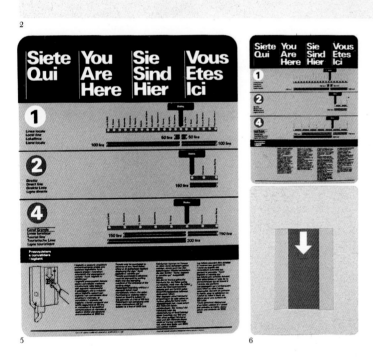

5

6

bergamin

Bergamin
Furniture department
store
Gruppo Signo
Communicazione Totale
Designer: Giulio Cittato
Venice, Italy

1

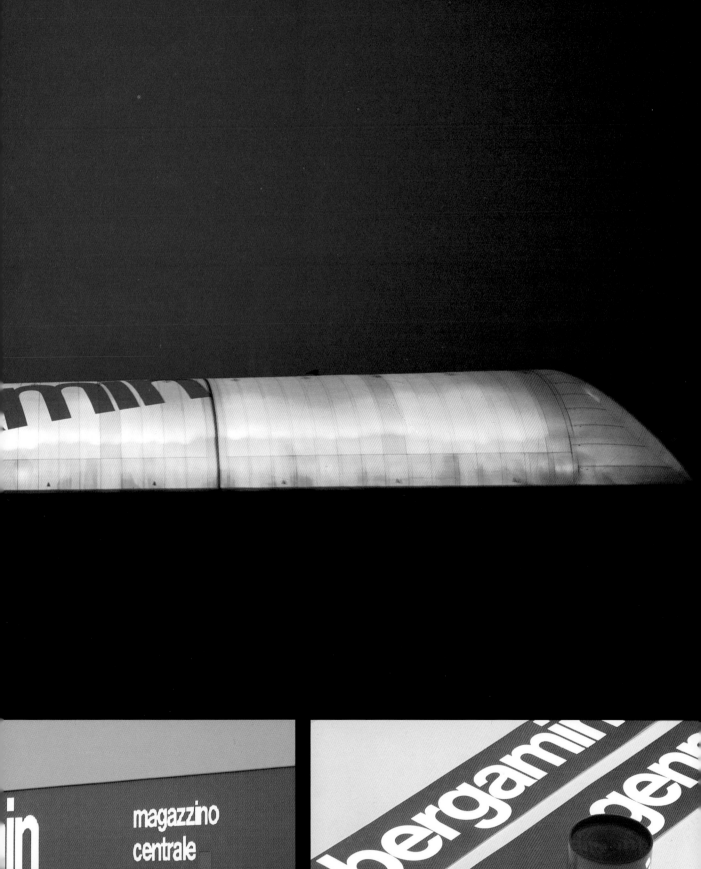

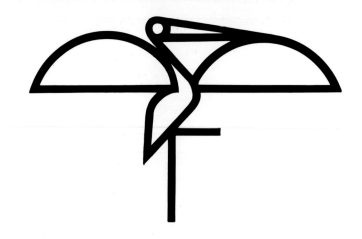

Lamperti
Cotton company
Studio Coppola
Designer: Silvio Coppola
Milan, Italy

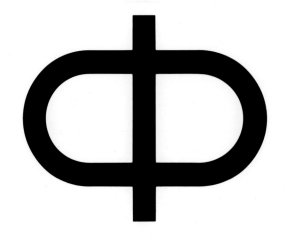

Prospero
Restaurant
Studio Coppola
Designer: Silvio Coppola
Milan, Italy

Tigammon
Lighting fixtures and
fittings
Studio Coppola
Designer: Silvio Coppola
Milan, Italy

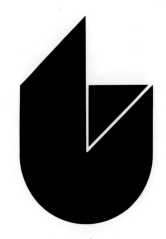

Parmalat
Milk products
Studio Coppola
Designer: Silvio Coppola
Milan, Italy

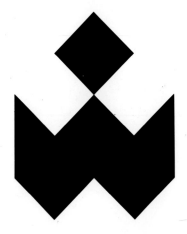

Ceramica Falcinelli
Decorative ceramics
Franco Grignani
Designer: Franco Grignani
Milan, Italy

Carpenfin
Carpet manufacturers
Franco Grignani
Designer: Franco Grignani
Milan, Italy

**Fedeazione Italiana
della Pubblicitá**
Italian Federation of
Publicity
Franco Grignani
Designer: Franco Grignani
Milan, Italy

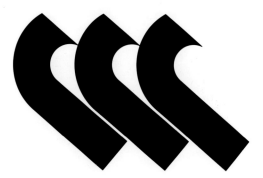

Marcon IV
Gallery of Modern Art
Franco Grignani
Designer: Franco Grignani
Milan, Italy

Cinquini
Shirt factory
Franco Grignani
Designer: Franco Grignani
Milan, Italy

Delchi
Air conditioner
manufacturer
Franco Grignani
Designer: Franco Grignani
Milan, Italy

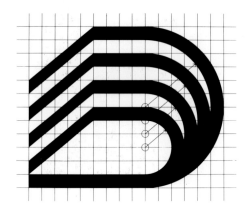

Aer Hotel
Travel agency
Franco Grignani
Designer: Franco Grignani
Milan, Italy

Nonopiano
Study center for the arts
Franco Grignani
Designer: Franco Grignani
Milan, Italy

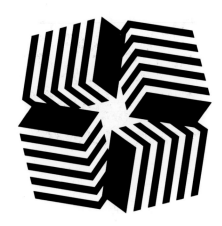

Cremona Nuova
Newspaper
Franco Grignani
Designer: Franco Grignani
Milan, Italy

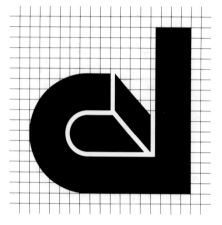

**Museum of Progressive
Contemporary Art**
Franco Grignani
Designer: Franco Grignani
Milan, Italy

Alpi
Science of information
organization
Franco Grignani
Designer: Franco Grignani
Milan, Italy

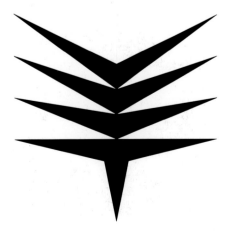

Helicopter Breda Nardi
Franco Grignani
Designer: Franco Grignani
Milan, Italy

Assopiastrelle
Clay tile manufacturers
Michele Spera
Designer: Michele Spera
Rome, Italy

1

2

3

4

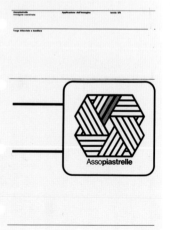

5

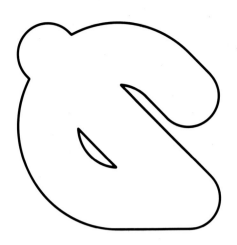

Lanificio Giuseppe Gatti
Wool and cotton
manufacturers
Michele Spera
Designer: Michele Spera
Rome, Italy

lanificio Giuseppe Gatti

Italian Radio and Television
Michele Spera
Designer: Michele Spera
Rome, Italy

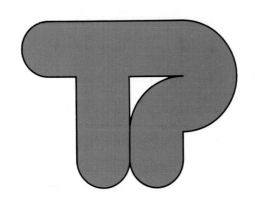
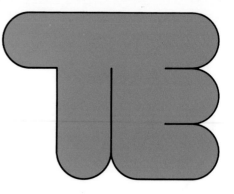
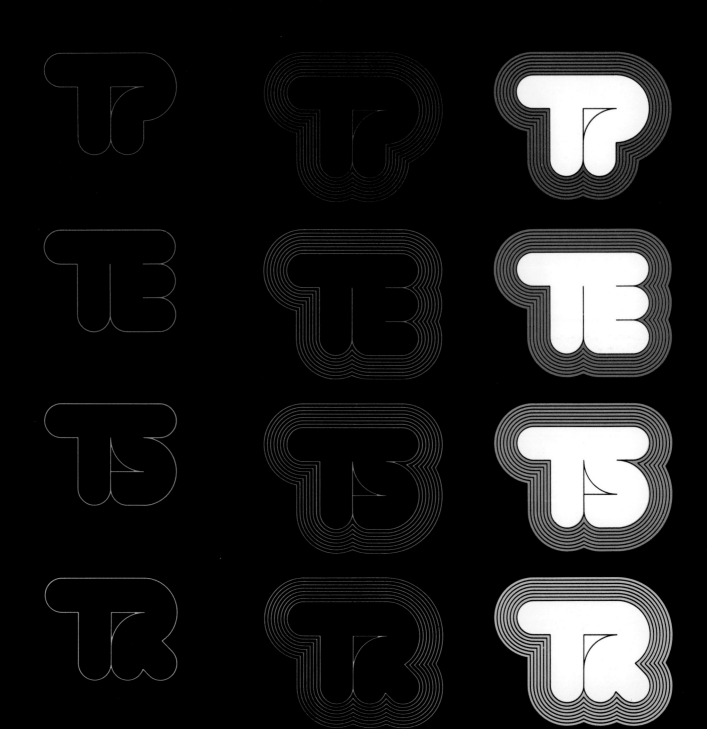

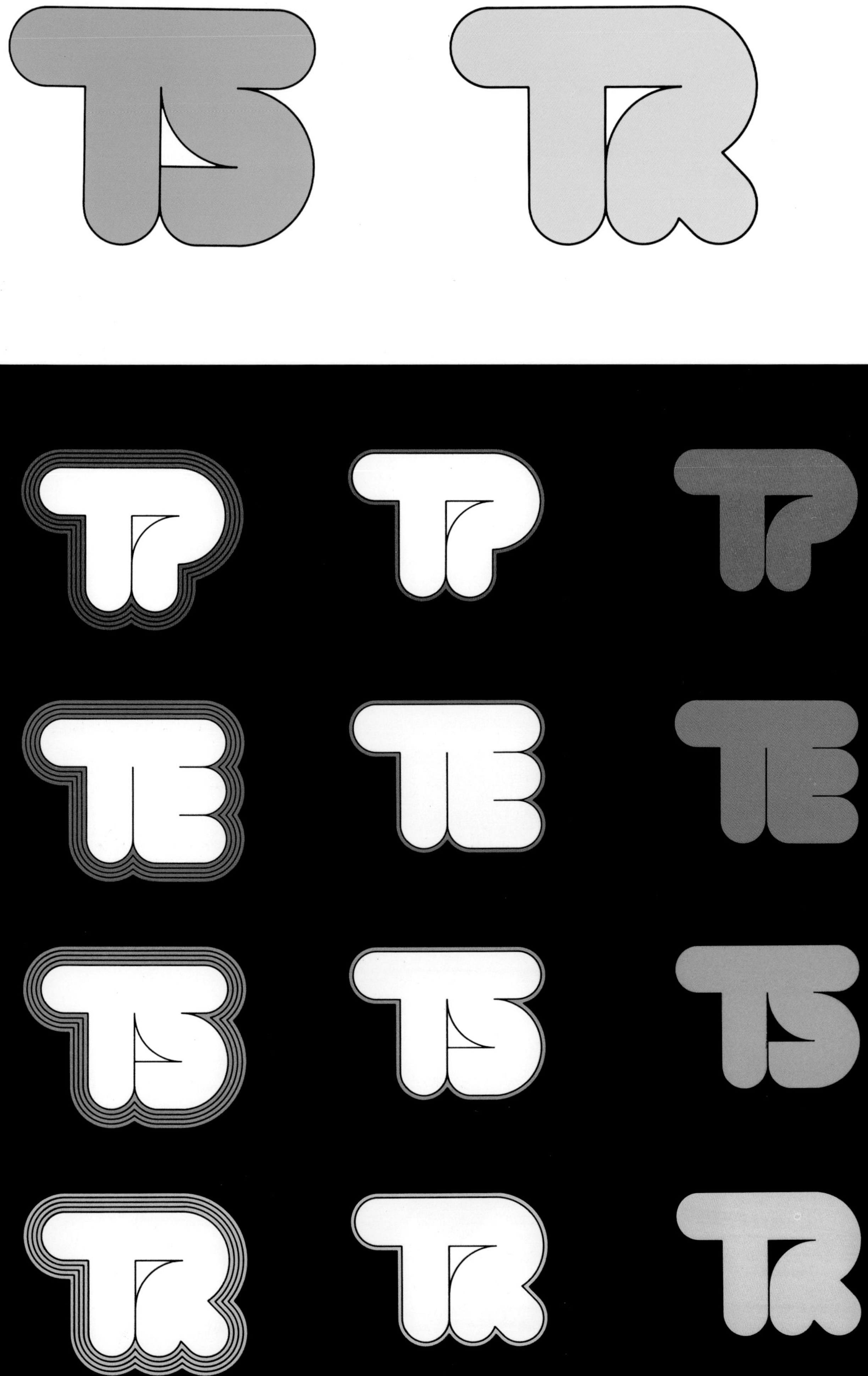

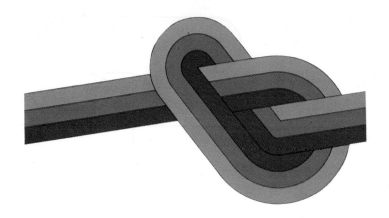

AGCI
Associazione Generale
Cooperative Italiane
Michele Spera
Designer: Michele Spera
Rome, Italy

AGCI
Associazione Generale
Cooperative Italiane

Il simbolo

tavola 1/4

Il simbolo al negativo
con il colore istituzionale

Una buona utilizzazione del simbolo
si ha ribaltando il colore
istituzionale dal simbolo stesso al fondo
che lo ospita. In questo caso otteniamo
il simbolo in negativo sul colore
istituzionale rif. 154.

AGCI
Associazione Generale
Cooperative Italiane

Il simbolo

tavola 1/11

Il simbolo e sue varianti
nell'applicazione di immagine
coordinata

Il simbolo AGCI è stato progettato in una
versione base per tutte le utilizzazioni
di uso corrente ed una serie di alternative
per applicazioni particolari.
Questa tavola riassume i vari simboli
ed il loro uso. Per la fotoriproduzione
degli stessi si rimanda alle tavole
specifiche relative agli argomenti trattati.
1. Simbolo base in nero
2. Simbolo base in colore
3. Simbolo a secco per le carte di
rappresentanza
4. Simbolo filettato, versione speciale
5. Simbolo filettato con colori
6. 7. 8. Varianti del simbolo per
utilizzazioni su diplomi, targhe, adesivi.

1

2

AGCI
Associazione Generale
Cooperative Italiane

Il simbolo

tavola 1/8

Iterazione del simbolo

Il simbolo dell'AGCI è costruito in modo
da poter essere ripetuto in successione
senza soluzione di continuità grazie
all'allineamento sulla linea orizzontale a-b.
L'assemblaggio di più simboli accentua
e moltiplica i contenuti che il simbolo
esprime ed offre una soluzione di grande
impatto visivo e di continuità.
I manifesti murali potrebbero essere un
ottimo strumento per l'utilizzazione del
simbolo iterato in una campagna
istituzionale sul marchio.

AGCI
Associazione Generale
Cooperative Italiane

Targhe/medaglie

tavola 6/1

Targhe a muro

Realizzate in acciaio spazzolato da
mm. 4 di spessore. Scritte e simboli incisi
e verniciati rispettivamente in nero e in
colore rif. 154. La targa in alto è destinata
all'affissione fuori dal portone d'ingresso
della sede dell'AGCI e reca l'indicazione
del piano. Ha una base uguale a quella
prevista per il suo scorrimento nelle guide
predisposto.
La targa in basso va sistemata sulla porta
d'ingresso al piano ed è supportata da
quattro viti a legno.

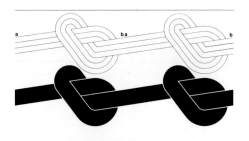

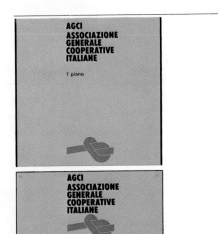

3

4

olivetti

Olivetti
Typewriter, personal
computer, and the
telematic field
Unidesign
Designer: Walter Ballmer
Milan, Italy

NAVA

Nava
Printing plant
Unidesign
Designer: Walter Ballmer
Milan, Italy

valentino

Valentino
Couturier
Unidesign
Designer: Walter Ballmer
Milan, Italy

Kitai
Unidesign
Designer: Walter Ballmer
Milan, Italy

KITAi

Netherlands

American Graffiti
Art gallery
Form Mediation
International
Designer: Pieter Brattinga
Amsterdam, Netherlands

AMERICAN GRAFFITI

Berenstraat 20
1016 GH Amsterdam
The Netherlands
Tel: 020-27 63 43

Handelsregister KvK
Amsterdam 156.500

ABN Bank
Minervaplein 18
Amsterdam
Account number
544742702

Raad
vanState

Raad van State
Council of the Dutch
Government
Government Printing
Office
Designers: Vincent Bus,
Rovert-Jan Hofhuis,
Fred van der Zee
Gravenhage, Netherlands

The Raad van State has
two branches: One advices
between civilians or civil
organizations and the
Dutch Government, the
other one is the highest
instance which passes
judgement in courts
against disposal of the
Goernment.

Raad
vanState

Postbus 20019
2500 EA 's-Gravenhage
Telefoon (070) 62 46 71

Afdeling voor de geschillen van bestuur

| Datum | Uw brief | Ons kenmerk | Afdeling |
| Onderwerp | | Bijlage(n) | |

Bezoekadres: Kneuterdijk

Bij correspondentie de datum van deze brief en
het kenmerk vermelden

01 - 30966ILC

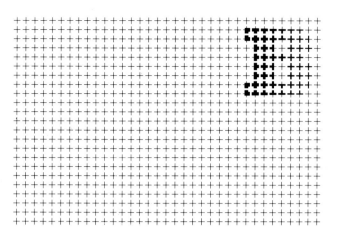

Ministry of Home Affairs
Government Printing Office, BRS Amsterdam
Designers: Floor Kamphorst,
Joost van Roon,
Jelle van der Toorn Vrijthoff
Gravenhage, Netherlands

Ministry of Home Affairs is one of the oldest ministries, established in 1813.
Home Affairs is the internal administration of the country, and the Ministry of Home Affairs is also which concerns itself with the terms and conditions of service of government employees, i.e. with the rights and responsibilities of all civil servants.

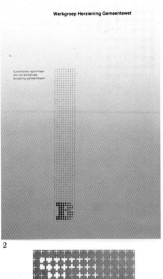

2

yvonne voogt

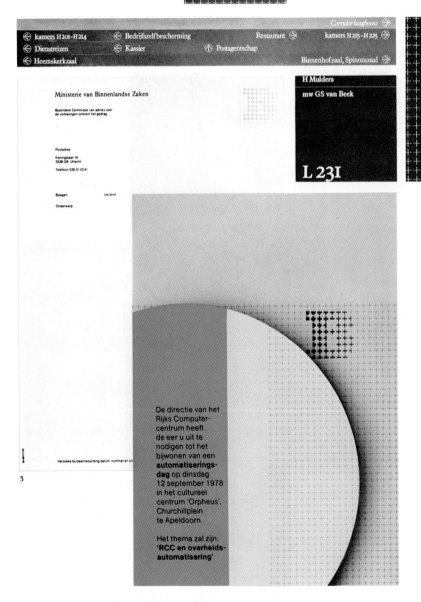

3

4

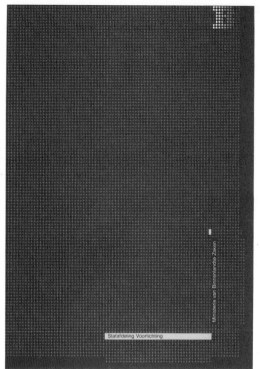

5

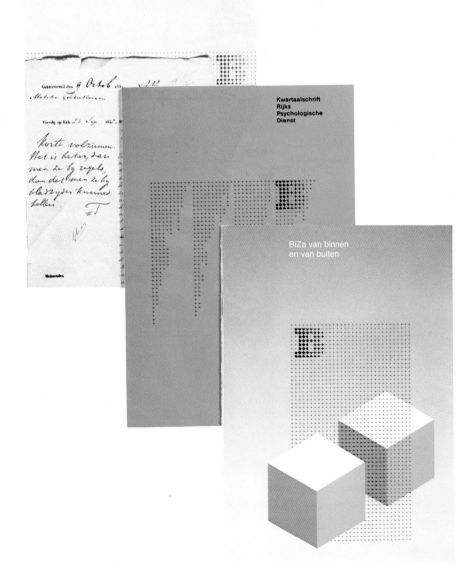

6

Telwerk

Telwerk
Graphic and industrial
design firm
Tel Design
Designers: Tel Design
The Hague, Netherlands

1

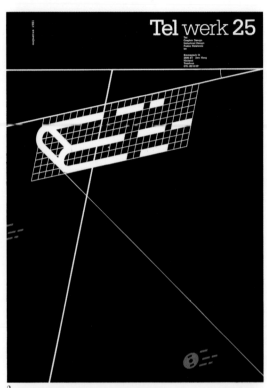

2

3

4

Info'Text

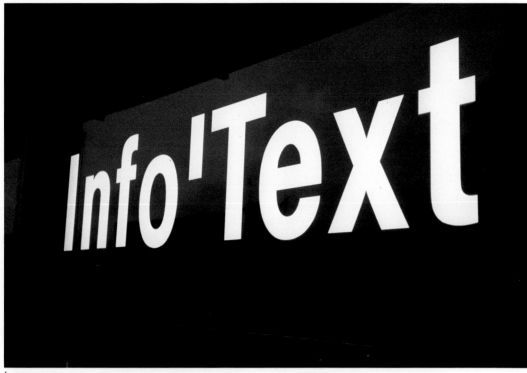

1

Info'Text
Computer services
Tel Design
Designers: Andrew Fallon,
Paul Vermijs
The Hague, Netherlands

Info'Text is a rapidly
expanding compnay
specializing in trading and
service of typewriters, data
processing equipment and
other computers. The
logotype consists simply
of two words connected by
an apostrophe.

Although the basic
logotype was designed in
condensed Helvetica
medium, other typefaces,
including typewriter and
VDU faces, may be used:
the apostrophe remains
characteristic even when
hand written. The same
method is used to relate
the company name to the
company products.

3

2

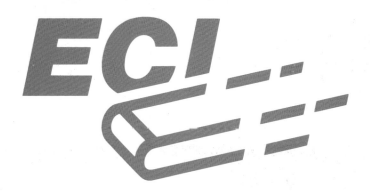

ECI
Book and record club
Tel Design
Designers: Will de l'Eluse,
Andrew Fallon,
Hans Verlaat,
Bobbert van Wezel
The Hague, Netherlands

ECI is the largest book and
record club in the
Netherlands and Belgium
with more than a million
members. The logotype
consists of the company
name in combination with
a pictogram of a book in
motion. Other words can
be used to replace the
company name and other
pictograms can be
similarly used instead of,
or inconjunction with the
book. The speed elements
(diagonal stripes and
dashes) and the 12° angle
are used together with the
company colors red and
blue to strengthen the
company's corporate
identity.

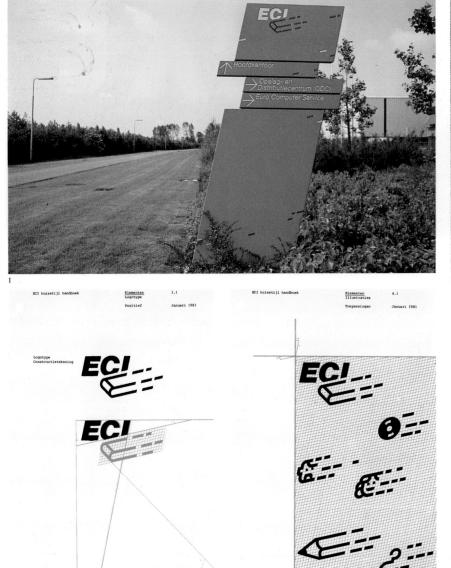

1

2

| ECI huisstijl handboek | Elementen
Logotype | 3.1 |
| | Positief | Januari 1981 |

| ECI huisstijl handboek | Elementen
Illustraties | 4.1 |
| | Toepassingen | Januari 1981 |

ECI huisstijl handboek

Logotype
Constructietekening

Logotype in dia-
positief gebruik
op zwarte achter-
grond

Logotype in dia-
positief gebruik
op zwarte achter-
grond met blauw
als steunkleur

4

5

6

Algemene Directie
Afdeling Personeelszaken
Afdeling Public Relations

3

ECI huisstijl handboek	Elementen Kleur	5.3
	Toepassingen	Januari 1981
ri 1981	Fond blauw	

ECI huisstijl handboek	Toepassingen ECI Boektiek lichtbak	10.1
		Januari 1981

ECI huisstijl handboek	Toepassingen Bewegwijzering	11.4
	Buiten	Juni 1981

Logotype in dia-
positief gebruik
op blauwe achter-
grond

Logotype in dia-
positief gebruik
op blauwe achter-
grond met rood
als steunkleur

Logotype in zwart
op blauwe achter-
grond

7

ECI BOEKTIEK

Lichtbak in voorkeurverhouding

ECI BOEKTIEK

Verlenging en verhoging van de lichtbak

Vierkante
lichtbak

Ontwerp ook te
gebruiken voor
deurduwer

ECI
BOEKTIEK

8

Detail tekststrook
pijl/typografie

Opslag- en
Distributiece

De teksten zijn op een Staromat gezet. De kapitaalhoogte is
50 mm. De spatiëring is een handspatiëring door Tel, bij een
eventuele aanvulling 1 : 1 voorbeeld opvragen.

Toepassing logo op
bovenvlak

ECI

Hoofdkantoor

Opslag- en
Distributiecentrum
Euro Computer Service

9

Capelle aan den IJssel
City of Capelle
Total Design
Designer: Ben Bos
Amsterdam, Netherlands

Capelle aan den IJssel is a
rapidly growing town
(50,000 inhabitants) near
Rotterdam. The new
symbol finds its back-
ground in the city's old
heraldry. The identity
program for this town is a
project which is still in
further development,
though much of it is
already visible.

Dronten
City of Dronten
Total Design
Designer: Ben Bos
Amsterdam, Netherlands

Dronten is a new town in
the land that Holland
reclaimed from Suydersea.
The symbol and an
identity program were
developed for promotional
activities to attract
industry and inhabitants.

B&G

B & G Hekwerk
Iron fencing manufacturer
Total Design
Designer: Ben Bos
Amsterdam, Netherlands

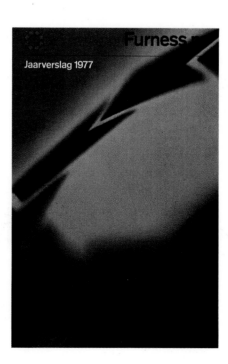

Jaarverslag 1977

Furness
Holding company
Total Design
Designer: Ben Bos
Amsterdam, Netherlands

Furness is a Rotterdam based holding company which operates divisions of stevedoring, shipowing, warehousing, transport, technical and trading activities, transport brokerage and insurance. The divisions all have their own symbol that consists of two or more flags in a specific configuration.

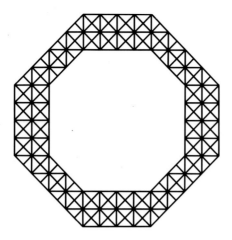

Groningen

City of Groningen
Total Design
Designer: Wim Crouwel
Amsterdam, Netherlands

The symbol for the twon
of Groningen is based on
a cross-section of the
Gothic tower, situated in
the middle of the city
which has played an
important role in the
history of the city.

Baskalis Westminster

Construction company
Total Design
Designer: Wim Crouwel
Amsterdam, Netherlands

The trademark for this
Dutch-British construction
and dredging company is
derived from the company
flag which developed from
a field which is divided
diagonally into a yellow
and blue field. This
division is expanded from
a square into a cube to
indicate the activities of
the company.

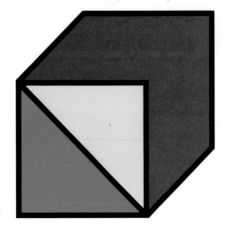

1

2

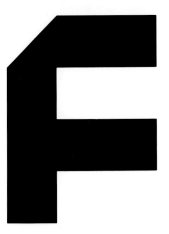

Friesland Bank
Total Design
Designer: Wim Crouwel
Amsterdam, Netherlands

The trademark for this
small agricultural bank in
the north of the
Netherlands is a solid
constructed capital F.

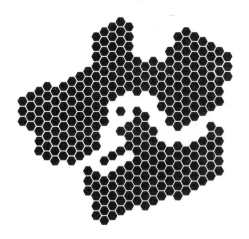

Rotterdam
Town of Rotterdam
Total Design
Designer: Wim Crouwel
Amsterdam, Netherlands

Spain

Venga. Entre. Mire.
Come Enter Look: Ad copy
Salvatore Adduci
Designer: Salvatore Adduci
Barcelona, Spain

**Venga.
Entre.
Mire.**

Chiminord
Silicone manufacturer
Salvatore Adduci
Designer: Salvatore Adduci
Barcelona, Spain

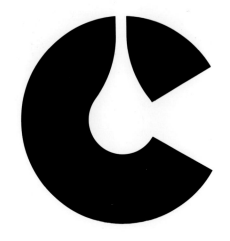

Santiveri
Dairy products
Enric Huguet
Designer: Enric Huguet
Barcelona, Spain

Santiveri

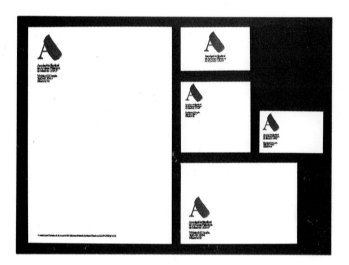

Asociación de Artistas Plásticos
Artists association
Fernando Medina Design
Designer: Fernando Medina
Madrid, Spain

El Cinematografo
Filmmaker
Fernando Medina Design
Designer: Fernando Medina
Madrid, Spain

ERTOIL
Lubricantes

Ertoil
Lubricant manufacturer
Fernando Medina Design
Designer: Fernando
Medina
Madrid, Spain

1

2

Bandarra
Self promotion
Russelot SA
Designer: Ricardo
Rousselot
Barcelona, Spain

José Luis Méndez
Photographer
Rousclot SA
Designer: Ricardo
Rousselot
Barcelona, Spain

The Parkview Wilshire
Hotel
Rousselot SA
Designer: Ricardo
Rousselot
Barcelona, Spain

John Follis
Graphic designer
Rousselot SA
Designer: Ricardo
Rousselot
Barcelona, Spain

America Sanchez
Graphic designer
America Sanchez
Designer: America
Sanchez
Barcelona, Spain

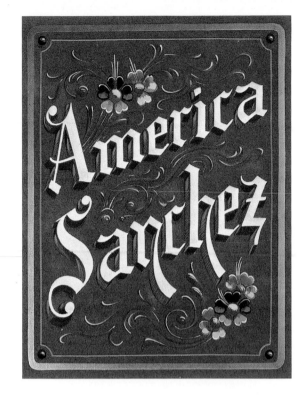

La Ceca
Theater
America Sanchez
Designer: America
Sanchez
Barcelona, Spain

L'envelat de La Ceca s.a. Flassaders 40 baixos Barcelona 3

Las Indias
Restaurant
Designer: America
Sanchez
Balcelona, Spain

312

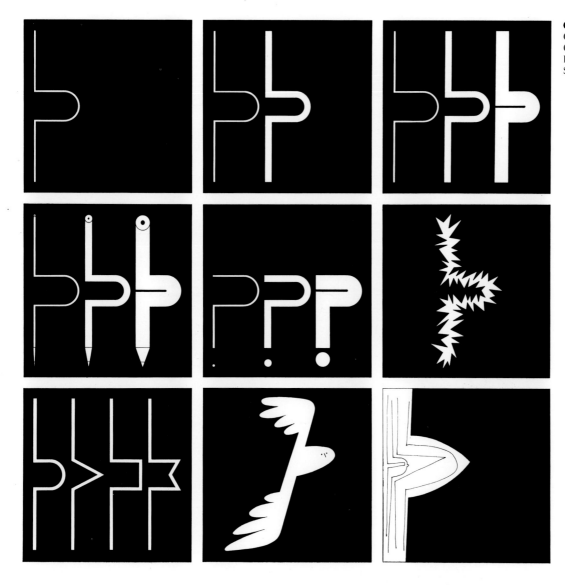

Olle Eksell Design
Graphic design studio
Olle Eksell Design
Designer: Olle Eksell
Stockholm, Sweden

Handelsbanken

Handelsbanken
Bank
Olle Eksell Design
Designer: Olle Eksell
Stockholm, Sweden

Banken har i praktiken två namn:
Svenska Handelsbanken och
Handelsbanken. Det ena är vårt
registrerade firmanamn, det andra
vårt namn i dagligt tal.

Vi bör använda de olika namnformerna
på ett enhetligt och konsekvent sätt,
och därför har bankledningen fastställt
följande riktlinjer.

1. Vi bör följa det normala språkbruket
och använda den kortare
namnformen i alla sammanhang
där det inte finns särskilda skäl
att skriva ut hela namnet.

Salunda kommer vi att använda
namnet Handelsbanken i huvudena
på vara blanketter, brevpapper och
checkar, liksom i allmän information,
annonser, trycksaker, affischer och
efter hand på vara fasadskyltar.

2. Däremot ska vi skriva ut hela namnet
Svenska Handelsbanken i sådana
sammanhang där vi i text eller
underskrift gör åtaganden
eller blir föremal för rättigheter.
(Beträffande brev se sidan 16.)

Vi ska också heta
Svenska Handelsbanken
i alla kontakter med utlandet.

Namnet ska alltid skrivas med gemena
(sma) bokstäver, utom initialerna.

När namnet förekommer i
löpande text, ska det sättas med
samma stil som övrig text.

Regionbanksnamnen, t ex Handelsbanken Norra Norrland, är huvud-
sakligen att betrakta som interna
beteckningar och inte som delar av
vårt namn. (Se t ex brevpapper,
sidan 15.)

Det finns ingen anledning att franga
förkortningen SHB i de sammanhang
där förkortning behövs.

1

Bankens nya logotype (namnbild) är
satt med stilen halvfet Helvetica.

Logotypen ska alltid användas när
bankens namn är fristående, t ex under
en annonstext och på ett brevhuvud.
I löpande text ska logotypen aldrig
förekomma, utan då används samma
stil som övrig text.

När logotypen ska användas, biloga
alltid original till tryckeriet.
Logotypekartor rekvireras från RHK.

Handelsbanken

2

Logotypen ska vara blå eller svart. Den
kan också tryckas negativt (vitt) på
blått och andra färger. Angående den
blå färgnyansen se sidan 10.

Handelsbanken

Handelsbanken

Handelsbanken

3

Logotypen bör ha en viss "luft"
omkring sig. För att bestämma
avstånden från logotypen till
omgivande text, marginaler, bilder etc
har vissa minimimått angetts,
som framgår av illustrationerna.

Som måttenhet har vi använt
bokstaven H i logotypen. Vid höjdmått
utgår man från höjden på H och vid
breddmått från bredden på H.

Logotypen bör placeras
i rak vänsterkant med övrig text.

Undvik reklamfraser och upplysningar
kring logotypen. Vill Du t ex ha med
adress, telefonnummer och öppetider
i en annons, så placera uppgifterna
i den löpande texten.

4

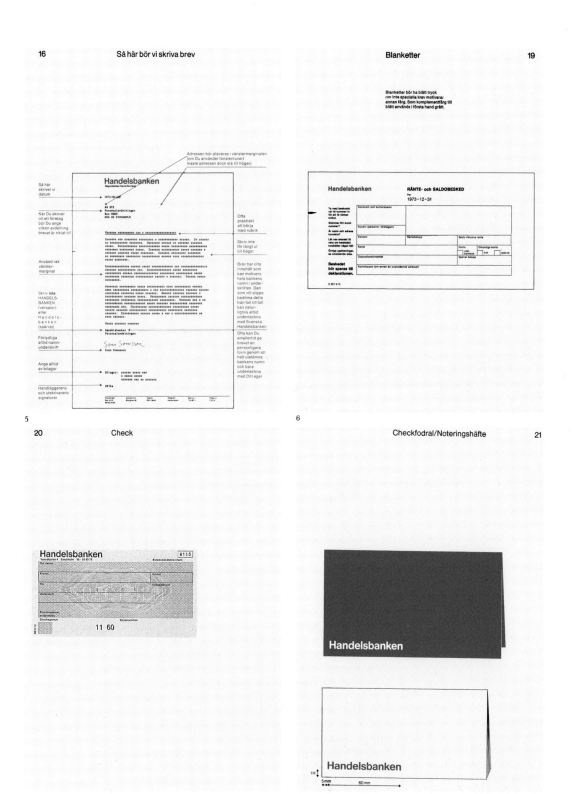

Blanketter bör ha blått tryck
om inte speciella krav motiverar
annan färg. Som komplementfärg till
blått används i första hand grått.

Adressen bör placeras i vänstermarginalen
(om Du använder fönsterkuvert
måste adressen dock stå till höger)

Handelsbanken

Så här
skriver vi
datum

När Du skriver
till ett företag
bör Du ange
vilken avdelning
brevet är riktat till

Ofta
praktiskt
att börja
med rubrik

Skriv inte
för långt ut
till höger

Använd rak
vänster-
marginal

Brev har ofta
innehåll som
kan motivera
hela bankens
namn i under-
skriften. Den
som vill slippa
bedöma detta
från fall till fall
kan natur-
ligtvis alltid
underteckna
med Svenska
Handelsbanken

Skriv inte
HANDELS-
BANKEN
(versaler)
eller
H a n d e l s -
b a n k e n
(spärrat)

Förtydliga
alltid namn-
underskrift

Ofta kan Du
emellertid ge
brevet en
personligare
form genom att
helt utelämna
bankens namn
och bara
underteckna
med Ditt eget

Ange alltid
ev bilagor

Handläggarens
och utskrivarens
signaturer

Handelsbanken   RÄNTE- och SALDOBESKED
Per
1973-12-31

Beskedet
bör sparas till
deklarationen.

5

6

Handelsbanken

6115

11 60

Handelsbanken

Handelsbanken

5 mm   60 mm

7

8

**Sveriges
Advokatsamfund**
Society of Swedish
lawyers
Olle Eksell Design
Designer: Olle Eksell
Stockholm, Sweden

Sveriges Advokatsamfund   *Posttidning*

Box 27321
102 54 Stockholm

08-24 58 70

§

AV Producenterna
Audio visual center
Olle Eksell Design
Designer: Olle Eksell
Stockholm, Sweden

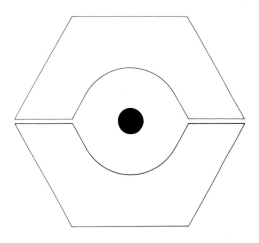

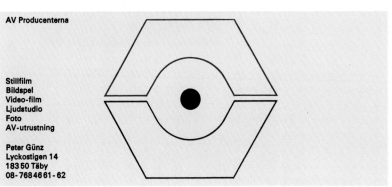

AV Producenterna

Stillfilm
Bildspel
Video-film
Ljudstudio
Foto
AV-utrustning

Peter Günz
Lyckostigen 14
183 50 Täby
08- 768 46 61 - 62

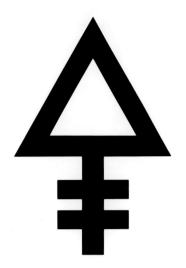

Supra
Chemical company
Olle Eksell Design
Designer: Olle Eksell
Stockholm, Sweden

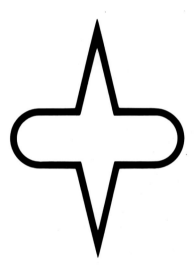

Nordverk
Industrial equipment
manufacturer
Olle Eksell Design
Designer: Olle Eksell
Stockholm, Sweden

Arjo
Hospital equipment
Olle Eksell Design
Designer: Olle Eksell
Stockholm, Sweden

Switzerland

Züri Metzgete
Bicycle race
Baltis und Rüegg
Designer: Bernadette
Baltis
Zürich, Switzerland

Mäser AG
Textile mill
Baltis und Rüegg
Designer: Ruedi Rüegg
Zürich, Switzerland

m/ä/s/e/r

Surselva
Baltis und Rüegg
Designer: Urs
Aschwanden
Zürich, Switzerland

Bündner Oberland

Airport-Forum
Meeting halls at the
Airport
Baltis und Rüegg
Designer: Ruedi Rüegg
Zürich, Switzerland

air✈port **forum**

Sprecher AG
Baltis und Rüegg
Designers: Ruedi Rüegg,
Peter Giovannini
Zürich, Switzerland

Sprecher

Pyria Heizkessel
Boilers
Baltis und Rüegg
Designer: Ruedi Rüegg
Zürich, Switzerland

Schweiz.
Geisteswissenschaftliche
Gesellschaft
Society of the humanities
Baltis und Rüegg
Designer: Ruedi Rüegg
Zürich, Switzerland

Sporthotel Stoos
Hotel
Baltis und Rüegg
Designer: Urs
Aschwanden
Zürich, Switzerland

Göhner AG
General contractor
Baltis und Rüegg
Designer: Ruedi Rüegg
Zürich, Switzerland

Forbo
Linoleum manufacturer
Geissbühler KD
Designers: Geissbühler
KD
Zürich, Switzerland

Stahel Hardmeyer
Cotton merchant
Geissbühler KD
Designers: Geissbühler
KD
Zürich, Switzerland

Otto Stadtlander
Cotton merchant
Geissbühler KD
Designers: Geissbühler
KD
Zürich, Switzerland

Cosa
Geissbühler KD
Designers: Geissbühler
KD
Zürich, Switzerland

Operahaus Zürich
Theater
Geissbühler KD
Designers: Geissbühler
KD
Zürich, Switzerland

1

2

3

C O S A

H. Frech
Engineering firm
Gottschalk + Ash
International
Designer: Fritz Gottschalk
Zürich, Switzerland

H Frech[SBII]
Ingenieurbüro
für Heizungs- und
Energietechnik

Buchholzstrasse 169
8053 Zürich
Telefon (01) 53 84 86

Ohne Brief an .

I/Ref. .
u/Ref. .

Betrifft   Datum

⌐ zu Ihren Akten   ⌐ zur Unterzeichnung   ⌐ kontrolliert zurück   ⌐ mit Bitte um Rückgabe
⌐ zur Kenntnisnahme   ⌐ zur Bezahlung   ⌐ unterzeichnet zurück   ⌐ gem. tel. Besprechung
⌐ zur Stellungnahme   ⌐ zur Weiterleitung   ⌐ mit Dank zurück   ⌐ gem. Ihrem Schreiben
⌐ zur Offertstellung   ⌐ zur Weiterbehandlung   ⌐ auf Ihren Wunsch   ⌐ _____
⌐ zur Prüfung/Kontrolle   ⌐ zur Erledigung   ⌐ mit Bitte um Anruf   ⌐

Beilagen

Bemerkungen

Mit freundlichen Grüssen

BM
Galerie Bruno Meissner
Gottschalk + Ash
International
Designer: Fritz Gottschalk
Zürich, Switzerland

322

24-Stunden-
Selbstbedienungs-
bank

ST.GALLISCHE KANTONALBANK

1

Sesam
St. Gallische Kantonal Bank
Gottschalk + Ash
International
Designer: Fritz Gottschalk
Zürich, Switzerland

Wenn Sie Geld abheben wollen, drücken Sie die blaue Taste

Auszahlung
Sie erfolgt in 100-Franken- und 20-Franken-Noten. Die Bezugssumme muss also mit 100 oder 20 teilbar sein. Sie heben beispielsweise Fr. 360.– ab. Dann bitte eintasten:
   3 6 0 , 0 0
Wenn auf dem Bildschirm der von Ihnen gewünschte Betrag richtig erscheint, schliessen Sie die Eingabe ab, indem Sie die grüne Taste drücken:

Eingabe bestätigen
Nun können Sie – nach den Anweisungen auf dem Bildschirm – zuerst die Karte und dann das Geld herausnehmen.
   8

2

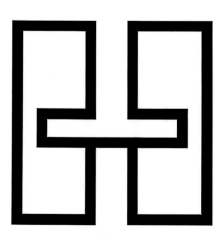

Hascott
Financial management
firm
Gottschalk + Ash
International
Designer: Fritz Gottschalk
Zürich, Switzerland

Gruppe **21**

Europäische Form

Gruppe 21
Glassware company
Müller-Brockman & Co.
Designers: Josef Müller-
Brockman & Co.
Zürich, Switzerland

1

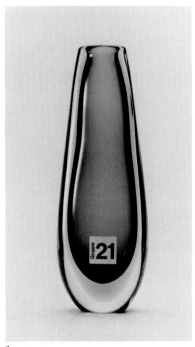

2

3

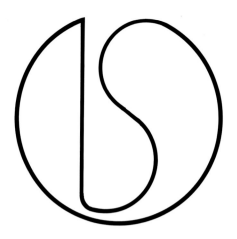

Vallotton   Böcklin   Amiet
Autel (Disentis)   Gleyre   Taeuber-Arp
Werner   Madone (Saas) Autel (Fribourg)

Nous,

l'art suisse–

et vous?

**Schweizerisches Institut
für Kunstwissenschaft**
Swiss Institute for Art
Research
Müller-Brockman & Co.
Designers: Josef Müller-
Brockman & Co.
Zürich, Switzerland

1

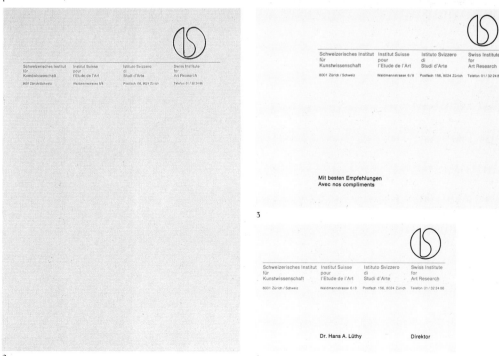

Schweizerisches Institut   Institut Suisse   Istituto Svizzero   Swiss Institute
für   pour   di   for
Kunstwissenschaft   l'Etude de l'Art   Studi d'Arte   Art Research

8001 Zürich/Schweiz   Waldmannstrasse 8/8   Postfach 156, 8024 Zürich   Telefon 01 / 32 24 86

Schweizerisches Institut   Institut Suisse   Istituto Svizzero   Swiss Institute
für   pour   di   for
Kunstwissenschaft   l'Etude de l'Art   Studi d'Arte   Art Research

8001 Zürich / Schweiz   Waldmannstrasse 6 / 8   Postfach 156, 8024 Zürich   Telefon 01 / 32 24 86

Mit besten Empfehlungen
Avec nos compliments

3

Schweizerisches Institut   Institut Suisse   Istituto Svizzero   Swiss Institute
für   pour   di   for
Kunstwissenschaft   l'Etude de l'Art   Studi d'Arte   Art Research

8001 Zürich / Schweiz   Waldmannstrasse 6 / 8   Postfach 156, 8024 Zürich   Telefon 01 / 32 24 86

Dr. Hans A. Lüthy   Direktor

2

4

-weishaupt-

Weishaupt
Industrial equipment
Müller-Brockman & Co.
Designers: Josef Müller-
Brockman & Co.
Zürich, Switzerland

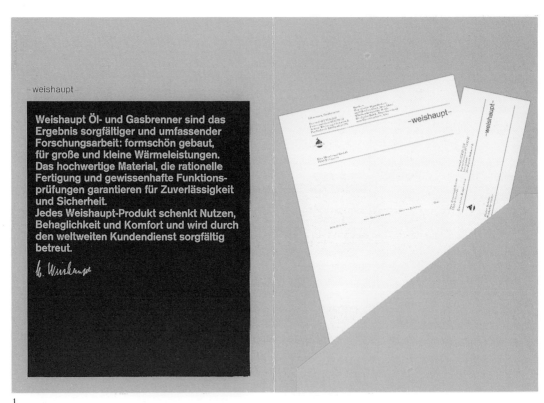

-weishaupt-

Weishaupt Öl- und Gasbrenner sind das
Ergebnis sorgfältiger und umfassender
Forschungsarbeit: formschön gebaut,
für große und kleine Wärmeleistungen.
Das hochwertige Material, die rationelle
Fertigung und gewissenhafte Funktions-
prüfungen garantieren für Zuverlässigkeit
und Sicherheit.
Jedes Weishaupt-Produkt schenkt Nutzen,
Behaglichkeit und Komfort und wird durch
den weltweiten Kundendienst sorgfältig
betreut.

1

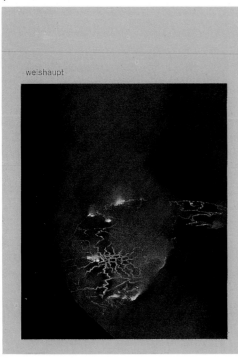

weishaupt

Weishaupt-Gasbrenner Typ G
Zweistoffbrenner Öl/Gas Typen GL und RGL
Baugrößen 5 bis 11

-weishaupt-

2   3

Das Werk

Führendes Forschungsinstitut

Grundlage eines führenden, modernen Unternehmens ist Forschung. Dank intensivster Entwicklungsarbeit ist Weishaupt heute eines der führenden Unternehmen der Feuerungstechnik. Das war gestern so, ist heute so und wird es auch in der Zukunft bleiben.

Was in unserem Forschungsinstitut als richtig und zukunftsweisend erkannt wird, nimmt in modernsten Produktionsstätten Form und Gestalt an. Über 1000 Menschen, jeder an seinem Platz, schaffen qualitativ hochwertige Produkte: Ölbrenner, Gasbrenner, Zweistoffbrenner Gas/Öl und Schaltanlagen. Über 1 Million Brenner erfüllen schon ihre Aufgabe, mehr als 100000 kommen zur Zufriedenheit unserer Auftraggeber jedes Jahr dazu. Als Ergebnis beständiger Zusammenarbeit zwischen modernster Forschung und Produktion.

Kundendienst

Schnell und zuverlässig

Weishaupt-Service, vertraglich gesichert

Service-Stellen, überall im Lande

Weishaupt-Service-Techniker, immer zur Stelle

Typisch für Weishaupt: die gelb-weißen Kundendienstwagen

Der Weishaupt-Kunden-Service steht immer zur Verfügung. Und das rund um die Uhr, schnell und zuverlässig.

Dafür sorgen eine große Anzahl fachkundiger Heizungsfirmen, welche Weishaupt-Brenner montieren und warten. Dafür sorgt auch das engmaschige Weishaupt-Service-Netz. Über 150 Kundendienststellen sind zum Einsatz bereit, mit rund 700 Servicewagen, wovon eine ganze Reihe mit Funk ausgerüstet sind.

Der Weishaupt-Kunden-Service ist die Ergänzung zum hochwertigen Weishaupt-Produkt: das Dienstleistungspaket ist komplett.

4

—weishaupt—   **Wer wir sind.**   **Was wir tun.**

5

UNION

Union
Textile manufacturer
Odermatt & Tissi
Designer: Siegfried
Odermatt
Zürich, Switzerland

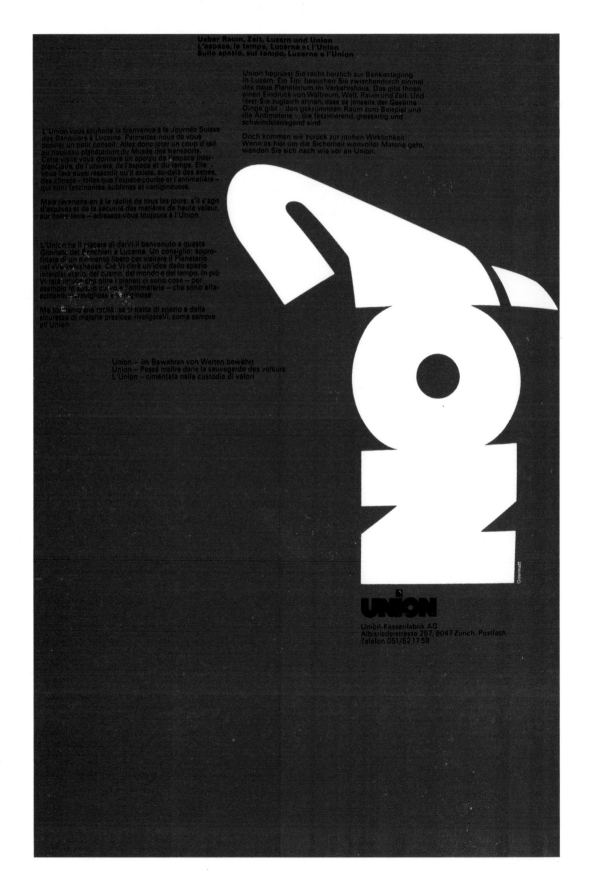

Ueber Raum, Zeit, Luzern und Union
L'espace, le temps, Lucerne et l'Union
Sullo spazio, sul tempo, Lucerna e l'Union

Union begrüsst Sie recht herzlich zur Bankiertagung in Luzern. Ein Tip: besuchen Sie zwischendurch einmal das neue Planetarium im Verkehrshaus. Das gibt Ihnen einen Eindruck von Weltraum, Welt, Raum und Zeit. Und lässt Sie zugleich ahnen, dass es jenseits der Gestirne Dinge gibt – den gekrümmten Raum zum Beispiel und die Antimaterie –, die faszinierend, grossartig und schwindelerregend sind.

Doch kommen wir zurück zur rauhen Wirklichkeit: Wenn es hier um die Sicherheit wertvoller Materie geht, wenden Sie sich nach wie vor an Union.

L'Union vous souhaite la bienvenue à la Journée Suisse des Banquiers à Lucerne. Permettez-nous de vous donner un petit conseil: Allez donc jeter un coup d'œil au nouveau planétarium du Musée des transports. Cette visite vous donnera un aperçu de l'espace interplanétaire, de l'univers, de l'espace et du temps. Elle vous fera aussi ressentir qu'il existe, au-delà des astres, des choses – telles que l'espace courbe et l'antimatière – qui sont fascinantes, sublimes et vertigineuses.

Mais revenons-en à la réalité de tous les jours: s'il s'agit d'espaces et de la sécurité des matières de haute valeur, sur notre terre – adressez-vous toujours à l'Union.

L'Union ha il piacere di darVi il benvenuto a questa Giornata dei Banchieri a Lucerna. Un consiglio: approfittate di un momento libero per visitare il Planetario nel «Verkehrshaus». Ciò Vi darà un'idea dello spazio interplanetario, del cosmo, del mondo e del tempo. In più Vi farà intuire che oltre i pianeti ci sono cose – per esempio lo spazio curvo e l'antimateria – che sono affascinanti, meravigliose e vertiginose.

Ma torniamo alla realtà: se si tratta di spazio e della sicurezza di materie preziose, rivolgeteVi, come sempre all'Union.

Union – im Bewahren von Werten bewährt.
Union – Passé maître dans la sauvegarde des valeurs.
L'Union – cimentata nella custodia di valori.

UNION
Union-Kassenfabrik AG
Albisriederstrasse 267, 8047 Zürich, Postfach
Telefon 051/52 17 58

328

Geroldswil
Indoor swimming pool
Odermatt & Tissi
Designer: Rosmarie Tissi
Zürich, Switzerland

Sapt
Odermatt & Tissi
Designer: Siegfried
Odermatt
Zürich, Switzerland

SAPT

**Kupferschmid Papiere
en Gros**
Paper company
Odermatt & Tissi
Designer: Rosmarie Tissi
Zürich, Switzerland

Steiner & Wehrli
Flour mill
Odermatt & Tissi
Designer: Rosmarie Tissi
Zürich, Switzerland

datalink

Datalink
Computer systems
Odermatt & Tissi
Designer: Siegfried
Odermatt
Zürich, Switzerland

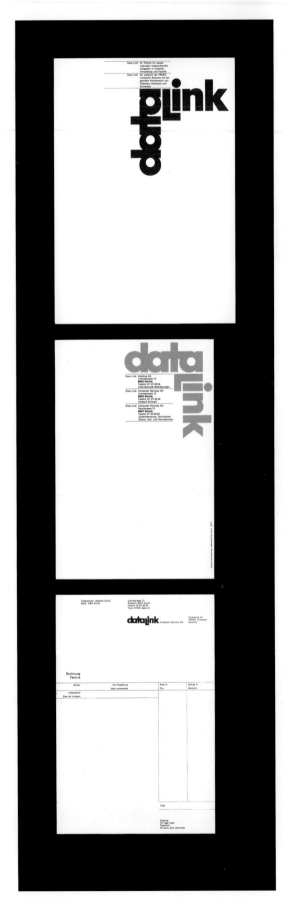

H. Bosshard
Architectural firm
Odermatt & Tissi
Designer: Rosmarie Tissi
Zürich, Switzerland

Architekturbüro
Hans J. Bosshard
Huebwiesenstrasse 34
CH-8954 Geroldswil
Telefon 01 748 05 53

Ihr Zeichen
Unser Zeichen
Geroldswil

Architekturbüro
Hans J. Bosshard
Huebwiesenstrasse 34
CH-8954 Geroldswil
Telefon 01 748 05 53

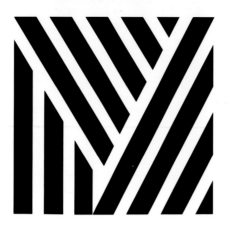

Mettler
Textile company
Odermatt & Tissi
Designer: Rosmarie Tissi
Zürich, Switzerland

1

2

3

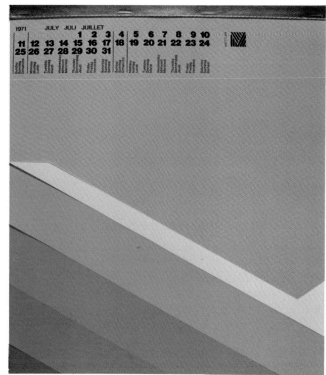

4

5

West Germany

V I D E O N

Videon
Video equipment and
services
Designer: Pierre Mendell
Mendell & Oberer
Munich, Germany

Videon is a German chain
of video rental stores and
a brand for blank video
tapes.

1

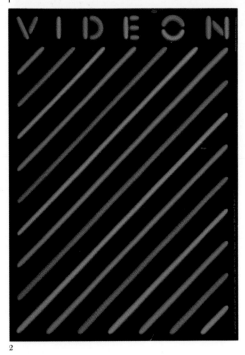

2

3

4

5

6

7

335

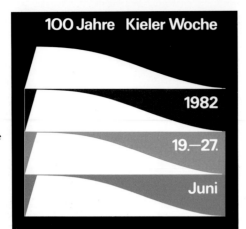

100 Jahre Kieler Woche
Yachting contest
BK Wiese Visual Design
Designer: BK Wiese
Hanburg, West Germany

2

3

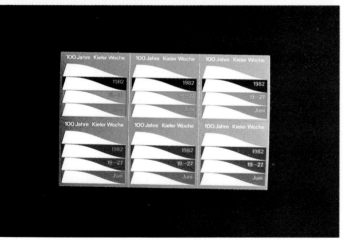

5

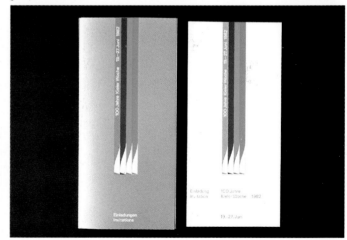

6

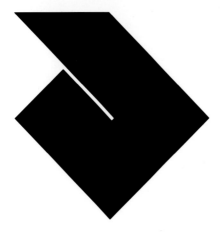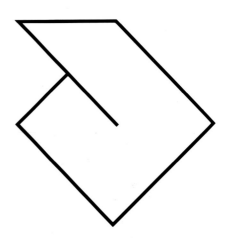

Deutscher Designertag
Association of German
graphic, industrial design
and photographers
BK Wiese Visual Design
Designer: BK Wiese
Hanburg, West Germany

Lotus
Tabacco company
BK Wiese Visual Design
Designer: BK Wiese
Hanburg, West Germany

1

2

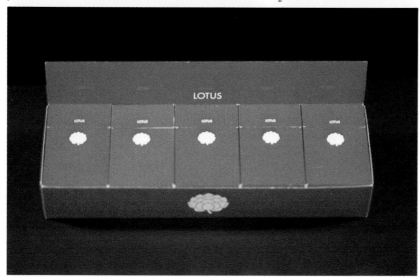

3

Chapter VI

Eastern Europe

Bulgaria

Czechoslovakia

Yugoslavia

Bulgaria

**Exposition Philatelique
Mondiale**
World stamp exposition
Designer: Stephan
Kantscheff
Sofia, Bulgaria

СВЕТОВНА ФИЛАТЕЛНА ИЗЛОЖБА
ВСЕМИРНАЯ ВЫСТАВКА ПОЧТОВЫХ МАРОК

ФИЛАСЕРДИКА '79·СОФИЯ
PHILASERDICA '79·SOFIA
18-27 МАЙ·MAI 1979

EXPOSITION PHILATELIQUE MONDIALE
WORLD STAMP EXHIBITION

ЗАЛИ:
УНИВЕРСИАДА
ФЕСТИВАЛНА
9-19 ЧАСА

SALLES:
UNIVERSIADA
FESTIVALNA
9-19 H.

1

342

2

ДЕН НА ТЕМАТИЧНОТО
КОЛЕКЦИОНИРАНЕ
27. 5. 1979

6

3

1904·1979

7

4

8

5

9

People's Palace of Culture, sofia 1980
Committee for culture
Designer: Stephan Kantscheff
Sofia, Bulgalia

Bulgaria Oceanography Exhibition Festival
Designer: Stephan Kantscheff
Sofia, Bulgaria

National Historic Museum Palace
Historic museum
Designer: Stephan Kantscheff
Sofia, Bulgaria

This symbol is derived from a combination of the lion, the contemporary symbol of the Bulgarian state, a spar and horse's tail. These images are from the original Proto-Bulgarian flag, representing 1300 years of Bulgarian history.

1

2

Crystalex
Glassworks
Designers: Vincenc Kutač,
Stanislav Kovář
Praha, Czechoslovakia

**Czechoslovakia Building
Industries Exhibition in
Moscow 1971**
Designer: Stanislav Kovář
Praha, Czechoslovakia

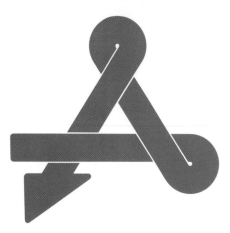

Design Around Us
Exhibition symbol
Designer: Vladislav
Rostoka
Bratislava, Czechoslovakia

Slovenská
národná
galéria

Bratislava

Kabinet
užitého
umenia a
priemyselného
designu

marec–
júl 1980

design
okolo
nás

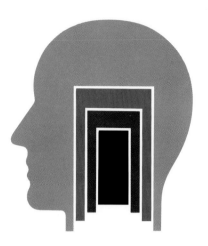

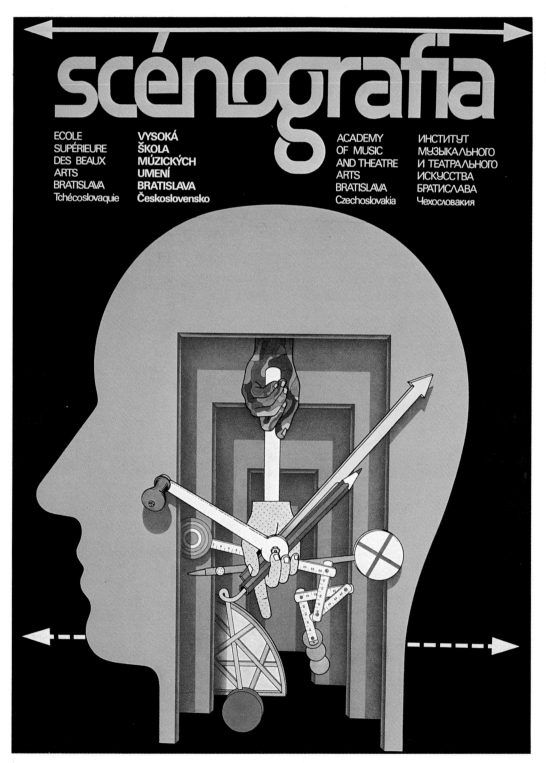

Scenography
Exhibition Symbol of
Academy and Theater
Designer: Vladislav
Rostoka
Bratislava, Czechoslovakia

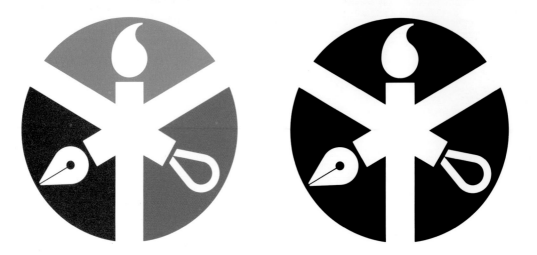

Young Gallery
Slovak Artists Association
Designer: Vladislav
Rostoka
Bratislava, Czechoslovakia

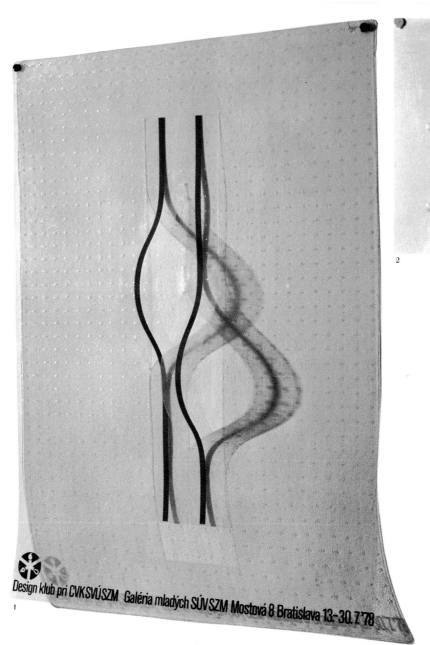

2

Design klub pri CVKSVÚSZM Galéria mladých SÚVSZM Mostová 8 Bratislava 13-30.7.'78

1

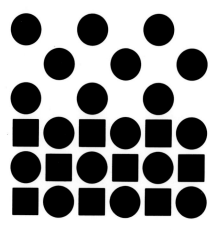

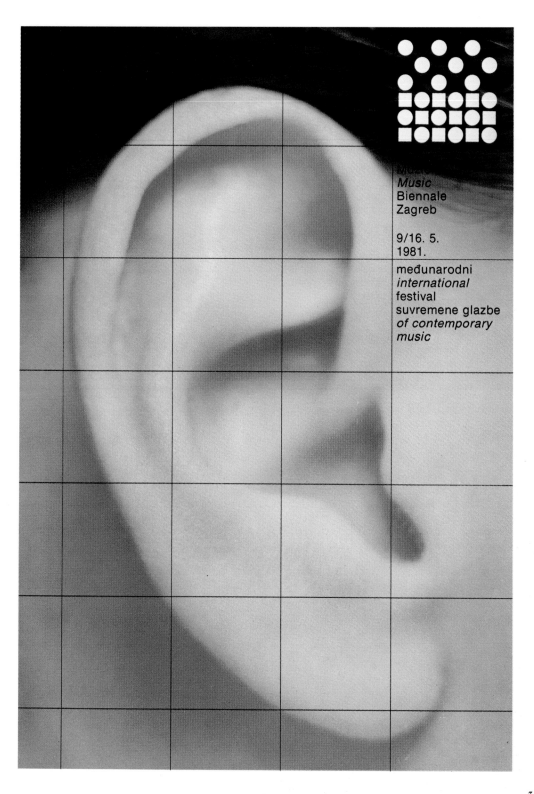

**Muzički Biennale
Zagreb'81**
International festival of
contemporary music
CIO
Designer: Borislav Ljubičić
Zagreb, Yugoslavia

The Zagreb Music
Biennale is a member of
the European Association
of Music Festivals. The
programme includes
music workshops, experi-
ments, a special presenta-
tion of Yugoslav music,
choral and orchestral concert rituals.

The 8th Mediterranean Games
Symbol of the game
Designer: Borislav Ljubičić
Zagreb, Yugoslavia

The Mediterranean Games
bring together fifteen
counties from shores of
the Meditterranean. The
symbol of these games
represents the motto of the
Games: sport, friendship
and peace in the Meditterranean.

1979 Calendar which was
awarded the best calendar
for 1979 in Yugoslavia,
designed by Borislav
Ljubičić, Stuart P. Hodges,
Stipe Brčić, photographed
by Mladen Tudor, Hrvoje
Knez.

1

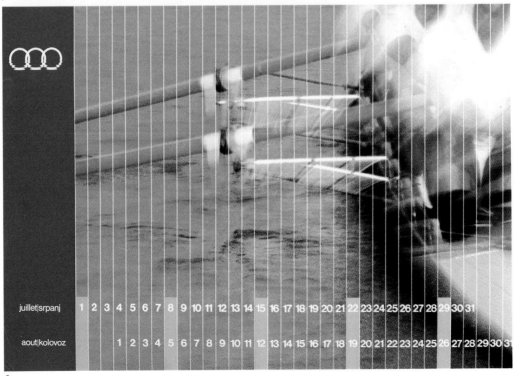

2

The 8th Mediterranean Games
Mascot symbol of the game
Oskar Kogoj International
Designer: Oskar Kogoj
Nova Gorica, Yugoslavia

The official mascot of the 8th Mediterranean Games is the sea bear, the species used to be widespread in the Mediterranean, but is now all but extinct because it caused damage to the fishermen's net. The main reason for the selection of the sea bear as the official mascot for the 8th Mediterranean Games was to draw the attention of the world public opinion and necessary ecological balance in the Mediterranean.

The official mascot was designed by Oskar Kogoj, member of the Visual Communications Team of the Centre for Industrial Design (CIT) for this project.

**Cestna Podjetja
Slovenije**
Designers: Ivan Dvoršak,
Matjaž Bertoncelj
Betnavska, Yugoslavia

Unial, Maribor
Designer: Ivan Dvoršak
Betnavska, Yugoslavia

Impol, Sloveska Bistrica
Metals industry
Designer: Ivan Dvoršak
Betravska, Yugoslavia

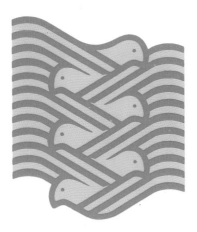

Fair of Friendship town
Dusán Jovanovič Studio
Designer: Dušan
Jovanovič
Koper, Yugoslavia

Obalne Galerije Piran
Coastal Galleries Piran
Dušan Jovanovič Studio
Designer: Dušan
Jovanovič
Koper, Yugoslavia

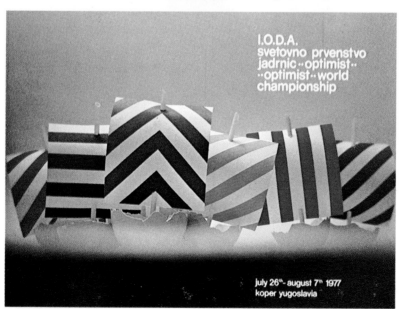

Optimist
World Championship
Koper 77
Dušan Jovanovič Studio
Designer: Dušan
Jovanovič
Koper, Yugoslavia

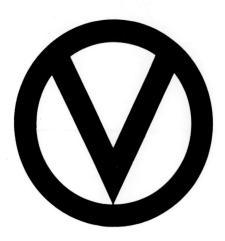

Vozila Gorica
Automobile industry
Oskar Kogoj International
Designer: Oskar Kogoj
Nova Gorica, Yugoslavia

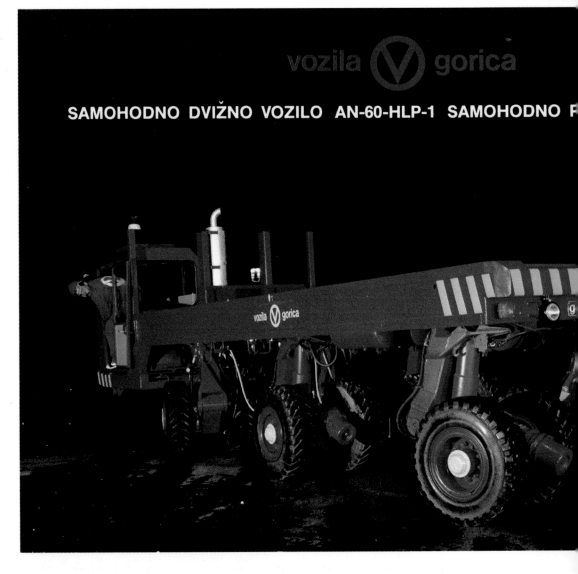

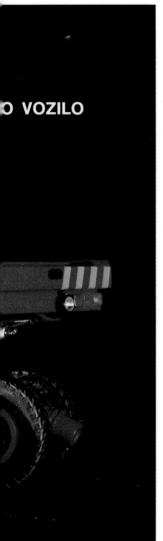

O VOZILO

Plastik
Plastics and metal
manufacturing
Oskar Kogoj International
Designer: Oskar Kogoj
Nova Gorica, Yugoslavia

Les
Furniture manufacturing
and wood production
Oskar kogoj International
Designer: Oskar Kogoj
Nova Gorica, Yugoslavia

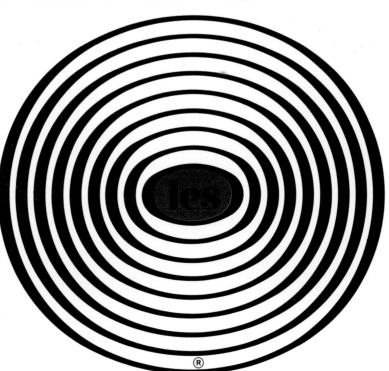

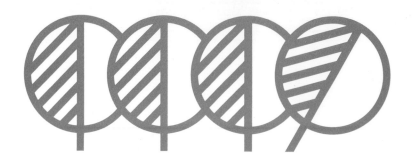

**The 16th Yugoslav
Foresters' Competition**
Designer: Katja Zelinka
Linhartova, Yugoslavia

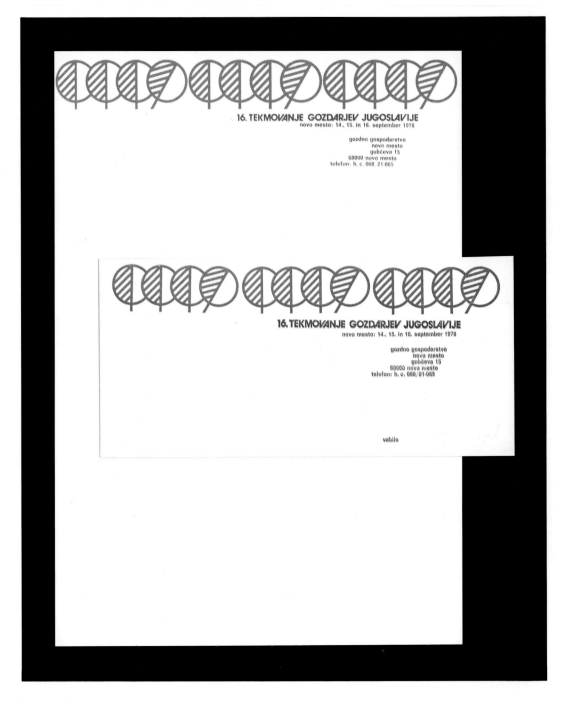

Naj Naj Cosmetics
Cosmetics
Designer: Katja Zelinka
Linhartova, Yugoslavia

Designers list

Project list

Designers address

Canada
Spencer/Francey (Fifty
Fingers Inc.)
236 King Street East
Toronto, ONT, M5A 1K1
416–869–3700

Gottschalk + Ash
International: Montreal
2050 Mansfield Suite 900
Montreal, QUE, H3A 1Y9
514–844–1995

Gottschalk + Ash
International: Toronto
322 King Street
Toronto, ONT, M5V 1J4
416–977–1879

Burton Kramer Associates
Ltd.
20 Prince Arthur Avenue
Suite 1E
Toronto, ONT, M5R 1B1
416–921–1078/3811

Mexico
Félix Beltrán Studio
Apartado de Correos
M-10733
México 0600 DF
382–43–32

Western United States
Primo Angeli Graphics
508 4th Street
San Francisco, CA 94107
415–974–6100

Saul Bass/Herb Yager &
Associates
7039 Sunset Boulevard
Los Angeles, CA 90028
213–466–9701

Design Collaborative
1824 NE Ravenna Boulevard
Seattle, WA 98105

Dyer/Kahn Inc.
5550 Wilshire Boulevard
Suite 301
Los Angeles, CA 90036
213–937–4100

John Follis & Associates
2124 Venice Boulevard
Los Angeles, CA 90006
213–735–1283

April Greiman
301 N Gower
Los Angeles, CA 90004
213–462–1771

Bruce Hopper Design
850 Dreier Street
Honolulu, HI 96813
808–942–1850

Landor Associates
Pier 5, Ferryboat Klamath
San Francisco, CA 94111
415–955–1200

Clarence Lee Design &
Associates Inc.
2333 Kapiolani Boulevard
Honolulu, HI 96826
808–941–5021

The Office of Michael
Manwaring
1005 Sansome Street
San Francisco, CA 94111
415–421–3595

Harry Murphy + Friends
224 Miller Avenue
Mill Valley, CA 94941
415–383–8586

Gerald Reis & Co.
185 Berry Street, #258
San Francisco, CA 94107
415–543–1344

Robert Miles Runyan &
Associates
200 E. Culver Boulevard
Playa del Rey, CA 90293
213–823–0975

Thomas & Associates
2238¹/₂ Purdue Avenue
Los Angeles, CA 90064
213–479–8477

Designfocus International
(Urano Design Inc.)
737 Bishop Street
Suite 1545
Honolulu, HI 96813
808–531–4681

Vanderbyl Design
Number 1 zoe Street
San Francisco, CA 94107
415–397–4583

The Weller Institute for the
Cure of Design Inc.
2427 Park Oak Drive
Los Angeles, CA 90068
213–467–4576

**Midwestern United
States**
Arthur Eisenberg Inc.
4924 Cole Avenue
Dallas, TEX 75205
214–528–5990

Hellmuth Obata &
Kassabaum
100 North Broadway
Saint Louis, MO 63102
314–421–2000

James Lienhart Design
58 West Huron
Chicago, IL 60610
312–565–0407

The names, addresses and telephone numbers of the following design firms fall in geographical order according to their country.

Loucks Atelier Inc.
2900 Weslayan Suite 530
Houston, TEX 77027
713-877-8551

Woody Pirtle Design
4528 McKinney Avenue
Suite 104
Dallas, TEX 75205
214-522-7520

Rodammer Morris
Associates
13140 Coit Road Suite 504
Dallas, TEX 75240
214-644-5259

Summerford Design Inc.
2706 Fairmount
Dallas, TEX 75201
214-748-4638

Eastern United States

Anspach Grossman
Portugal Inc.
711 Third Avenue
New York, NY 10017
212-692-9000

Bonnell Design Associates
Inc.
1457 Broadway
New York, NY 10036
212-921-5390

Cook and Shanosky
Associates Inc.
221 Nassau Street
Princeton, NJ 08540
609-921-0200

Rudolph de Harak &
Associates Inc.
150 Fifth Avenue
New York, NY 10011
212-929-5445

Milton Glaser Inc.
207 East + 32nd Street
New York, NY 10016
212-889-3161

Gottschalk + Ash
International: New York
170 Fifth Avenue
New York, NY 10010
212-807-0011

Willi Kunz Associates Inc.
2112 Broadway
New York, NY 10023
212-799-4300

David Leigh
1245 Park Avenue
New York, NY 10028
212-832-4770

Jonson, Pedersen, Hinrichs
& Shakery: New York
141 Lexington Avenue
New York, NY 10016
212-889-9611

Pentagram Design: New York
212 Fifth Avenue
New York, NY 10010
212-683-7000

Pushpin Lubalin Peckolick
67 Irving Place
New York, NY 10003
212-674-8080

Arnold Saks Associates
16 East 79 Street
New York, NY 10021
212-861-4300

Siegel & Gale
1185 Avenue of the Americas
New York, NY 10036
212-730-0101

George Tscherny Inc.
238 East 72 Street
New York, NY 10021
212-734-3277

Henry Wolf Productions Inc.
167 East 73 Street
New York, NY 10021
212-472-2500

Vignelli Associates
410 East 62 Street
New York, NY 10021
212-593-1416

Argentina

Arq. Gonzalez Ruiz
& Associates
Ricardo Rojas 401
esq. Leandro N. Alem/Piso
13
311-4684/3048

Brazil

Cauduro/Martino
Arquitetos Associados Ltda.
Rua Prof Vital Palma e Silva
131
01455 São Paulo SP
011-211-1911

Joaquim Redig
Estr. do Tambá 401/3/311
22450 Rio de Janeiro RJ
021-322-3383

DICV Design Ltda.
Rua Sampaio Vidal 159/41
01443 São Paulo SP
011-853-0405/852-7896

Hong Kong

Graphic Communication
Ltd.
28c Conduit Road
5-485548

India

Graphic Communication
Concepts
10 Sind Chambers
S. Bhagat Shingh Road
Colaba, Bombay – 400 005
217130-217637

Korea

Young Jae Cho Design
Studio
Apt 79-1305 Hyundae
Apkujung-Dong,
Kangnam-ku,
Seoul
542-5085

Israel

Dan Reisinger Designs
5 Zlocisti Street
Tel-Aviv 62994
03-266723/03-251433

Japan

Shigeo Fukuda
3-34-25 Kamikitazawa
Setagaya-ku, Tokyo 156
03-303-7806

Takenobu Igarashi Design
6-6-22 Minami-Aoyama
Minato-ku, Tokyo 107
03-498-3621

Yusaku Kamekura
Maison Hirakawa
2-5-2 Hirakawa-cho
Chiyoda-ku, Tokyo 102
03-264-4361

Kazumasa Nagai
Nippon Design Center
1-13-13 Ginza
Chuo-ku, Tokyo 104
03-567-3231

Paos INC.
5-5 Rokuban-cho
Chiyoda-ku, Tokyo 102
03-263-1331

Ikko Tanaka Design Studio
A.Y. Bldg.
3-2-2 Kita-Aoyama
Minato-ku, Tokyo 107
03-470-2611

Turkey
San Grafik
Cami Sokak Vğur
Ap. 44/46 Ayazpaşa
Istanbul
45 44 68 - 43 40 40 -
49 35 94

Australia
Bryce Design Consultants
212 Boundary Street
Spring Hill, Queensland
4000
07-221-4149

Ken Cato Design Co.
254 Swan Street
Richmond, Victoria 3206
429-6577

Emery Vincent Associates
46 Nicholson Street
South Yarra, Victoria 3141
26-1333

Fleet, Henderson & Arnold
217 Auburn Road
Hawthorn, Victoria 3123
03-429-6888

Goodwin Design
123 Harris Street
Pyrmont, NSW 2009
660-5384

Ian Hawksby
57 Downshire Road
Elsternwick, Victoria 3185
03-523-7693

Brian Sadgrove
6 Little Page Street
Albert Park, Victoria 3206
03-690-8977

New Zealand
Design Partners Ltd.
1 Grange Road Mt Eden
Auckland 3
603-809

Belgium
Paul Ibou
Legebaan 135
B-2260 Nijlen
031-481-82-94

Michel Olyff
Rue Haute 10
B-1461 Haut-Ittre
067-225794

Denmark
Papermint Design
Kompagnistraede 21
DK 1208 Copenhagen K
01-154845

England
WM de Majo Associates Ltd.
99 Archel Road
London W14 9QL
01-385-0394

Henrion, Ludlow & Schmidt
5-6 Clipstone Street
London W1P 7EB
01-636-1794

Lock/Pettersen Ltd.
56 Greek Street
London W1
01-439-6463

Minale, Tattersfield
& Partners Ltd.
Burston House,
Burston Road
Putney, London SW15 6AR
01-788-8261

Pentagram Design: London
61 North Wharf Road
London W2 1LA
01-402-5511

Michael Peters
& Partners Ltd.
4 Pembridge Mews, London
W11 3EQ
01-229-9476

David Pocknell Co., Ltd.
Readings Farm
Blackmore End Wethersfield
Essex
0787-61207

Wolff Olins
22 Dukes Road
London WC1H 9AB
01-387-0891

Finland
Studio G4
Aurorankatu 19A
00100 Helsinki 10
90-447-962

Kyösti Varis
ADV, Agency VPV Oy
Mannerheimintie 44A4
00260 Helsinki 26
440-644

Jukka Veistola
Veistola Oy
Tehtaankatu 34E
00150 Helsinki 15
170-566

France
Bureau d'Etudes Garamond
Guainville 28260 Anet
37-64-06-21

Gérard Guerre
20 Av des Gobelins
75005 Paris
1-337-6706

Jean Widmer
Visuel Design
126 boulevard A. Blanqui
75013 Paris
707-73-82

Italy
Giulio Cittato/Gruppo Signo
S. Elena Calle Oslavia 6
30122 Venezia
041-23435

Studio Coppola
Via Privata Perugia 10
20122 Milano
02-798-849

Franco Grignani
Via Biancadi Savoia 7
20122 Milano
598-449

Michele Spera
Via San Damaso 30
00165 Roma
636380

Unidesign
Via Revere, 16
20123 Milano
4694769

Netherlands
Form Mediation
International
Prinsengracht 628
1017 KT Amsterdam
020-22-42-65

Government Printing
& Publishing Office
Christoffel Plantijnstraat 2
P.O. Box 20014
2500 EA The Hague
3170789911

Tel Design
Emmapark 14
2595 ET The Hague
070-856305

TD Associatie voor Total
Design bv
Herengracht 567
1017 CD Amsterdam
020-24-74-96

Spain
Salvatore Adduchi
Dr. Roux, 127
Barcelona 17
93-205-00-11

Enric Huguet
Av. Gaudi 30
Barcelona 25
343-255-78-79

Fernando Medina Design
Santiago Bernabeu 6
Madrid 16
91-2618040

Rousselot SA
Sabino de Arana 28
Barcelona 28
93-339-78-50

America Sanchez
Dr. Roux 32
Barcelona 17
2046258

Sweden
Olle Eksell Design
Hedinsgata 15
S-11533 Stockholm
08-626233

Switzerland
Baltis & Ruegg
Klosbachstrasse 107
8030 Zürich
01/47-43-00

Geissbühler KD
Theaterstrasse 10
8001 Zürich
01/47-67-6

Gottschalk & Ash
International
Sonnhaldenstrasse 3
8032 Zürich
01/252-50-42

Muller Brockman & Co.
Enzianweg 4
8048 Zürich
01/491-40-22

Odermatt & Tissi
Schipfe 45
CH-8001 Zürich
01/211-94-77

West Germany
Mendell & Oberer
Widenmayerstr 12
8000 München 22
089-22-40-55

BK Wiese AG1 Visual
Design
D2 Hamburg
Allhornweg 7
040-603-89-82

Bulgaria
Stephan Kantscheff
Krastiu Sarafoff 17
1421 Sofia
65-18-22

Czechoslovakia
Stanislav Kováŕ
Narodni 32
110-00 Praha 1
224636

Vladislav Rostoka
Mateja Bela 8
CS-811 06 Bratislava
335-442

CIO
YU/41000 Zagreb
trg M. Tita 1/III
0038-41-44-81-24

Yugoslavia
Ivan Dvorsák
62000 Maribor
Betnavska 110
6224864

Duśan Jorvanovič Studio
Markora 33 Koper
066-25312

Oscar Kogoj
65291 Miren 122/b
Nova Gorica
065-54088

Katja Zelinka
Linhartova 9
61000 Ljubljana
061-324-458

World Trademarks and Logotypes

Editing and book conception	Takenobu Igarashi
Co-Editing	Ann Harakawa
Art direction	Takenobu Igarashi
Layout and Design	Takenobu Igarashi Design
	Ann Harakawa
	Hiromi Nakata
	Tomoharu Terada
	Kounosuke Fujii
Photographs	Hideki Adachi
	Seiji Ohtsuka
Cover photograph	Mitsumasa Fujitsuka
Translations	Shig Fujita
	GK Association
	Idioma Co., Ltd.
Typesetting	Hagiwara Printing Co., Ltd. HIPAL
Printing and binding	Toppan Printing Co., Ltd.
Responsible for publication	Toshirou Kuze
Co-ordinating	Seiki Okuda
Publisher	Graphic-sha Publishing Co., Ltd.
	1-9-12 Kudan-kita, Chiyoda-ku
	Tokyo 102, Japan
	Tel.: 03-263-4318

ISBN4-7661-0290-8